A Handbook for

Preparing Graduate Papers In Music

Second Edition

A Handbook for

Preparing Graduate Papers In Music

Second Edition

Prepared by

J. David Boyle, Professor Emeritus of Music Education and Music Therapy, University of Miami

Richard K. Fiese, Professor of Music, Houston Baptist University

Nancy Zavac, Librarian Associate Professor, University of Miami

Halcyon Press Ltd ★ Houston, Texas

Published by Halcyon Press, Ltd. http://www.halcyon-press.com

For information, write:

Halcyon Press, Ltd.
6065 Hillcroft Suite 525
Houston, TX 77081

Publication History
First Edition, April 2001
Second Printing, January 2002
Second Edition, March 2004

Library of Congress Cataloging-in-Publication Data

Boyle, J. David.
  A handbook for preparing graduate papers in music / prepared by J.
David Boyle, Richard K. Fiese, Nancy Zavac.-- 2nd ed.
    p. cm.
Includes bibliographical references.
  ISBN 1-931823-14-6 (alk. paper)
  1. Musicology--Handbooks, manuals, etc. 2. Academic
writing--Handbooks, manuals, etc. 3. Dissertations,
Academic--Handbooks, manuals, etc. I. Fiese, Richard K., 1957- II.
Zavac, Nancy, 1952-   . III. Title.
  ML3797.B68 2004
  808'.06678--dc22
                        2003021446

❖ *Contents* ❖

❋ 1 ❋
Introduction

Purpose

The purpose of this manual is to provide music students with guidelines to assist in the preparation of theses, essays, dissertations, and other papers that may be written as part of their graduate program. The manual includes information and examples for preparing such papers and is designed specifically to assist students in writing about music and in documenting references to music, music notation, recordings, and other musical resources. It is intended to complement guidelines provided by a university's graduate office and the two style manuals most used by music students, *A Manual for Writers of Term Papers, Theses, and Dissertations* (Turabian 1996) and the *Publication Manual of the American Psychological Association* (APA 2001).[1]

Chapter 1 provides three types of information: (a) descriptions of the various types of papers that students may be asked to write as part of their culminating experience for a graduate degree in music, (b) a perspective on the role and importance of scholarly inquiry in graduate study, and (c) general strategies to use in conducting a library search for historical, general background, relevant research, and other literature related to the particular topic. Chapter 2 describes two basic systems of documentation, discusses factors to consider in selecting a system, and examines some ethical issues related to documentation in scholarly writing. Chapter 3 stresses the importance of the research proposal, describes the major parts of a proposal, and offers guidelines to assist students through the proposal process. Chapter 4 provides information specific to the organization and preparation of master's recital papers. Chapter 5 suggests a general format for all graduate papers, outlines a basic system of headings, provides hints for dealing with some particular problems related to the frontispieces of a paper, and offers some guidelines for the use of *italics*, **bold**, and <u>underlining</u> and the inclusion of musical scores in a paper. Chapter 6 is designed to supplement the Turabian and APA style manuals by providing examples of documentation formats for use in citing musical scores, recordings, and electronic resources. Chapters 7 offers suggestions for enhancing a text through the use of simple music notation, and Chapter 8 provides guidelines for incorporating musical examples, tables, and figures into a paper.

Types of Papers

Besides term papers for particular courses, most graduate programs in a school or department of music require culminating experiences that involve a written document. These documents are variously called project papers, recital papers, theses, essays, or dissertations. While the primary emphasis often is on a project or recital, a written paper usually is required to document the event. The diversity of names for these papers is a result of several factors: (a) the nature of the academic program, (b) the nature of the culminating experience, (c) the extent, breadth, and/or depth of the program requirements for the culminating experience, and, to an extent, (d) tradition.

Theses, papers, and projects ordinarily are part of requirements for master's degrees, while essays and dissertations usually are names given to documents written by doctoral students. No doubt extensive papers could be written about the theoretical and philosophical underpinnings of the various definitions of the word *thesis*, but when the term is used in reference to graduate papers, it usually means a formal document written by candidates for a master's degree. A master's thesis usually employs a formal research methodology to test a certain hypothesis. Often a thesis will involve some type of experimental methodology, but other research methodologies, including descriptive, historical, or curricular development, may be employed. Many music theses make extensive use of analytical techniques. Therefore, the culminating writing project for master's programs in musicology, composition, music theory, music education, and music therapy is usually a thesis.

A *recital paper* essentially provides the documentation for a master's recital for students in performance areas, e.g., instrumental, keyboard, vocal, jazz instrumental, and jazz vocal performance. Obviously, the recital itself is the primary culminating experience for students in these programs, but the written document serves several purposes. Research about the works on the recital program is intended to provide insight into the music and its presentation. The recital paper documents the student's ability to (a) analyze music structurally, stylistically, and as it relates to performance and (b) communicate these ideas clearly.

A *project paper* is similar to a recital paper in that it provides the medium for documenting the culminating experience in a degree program requiring a project, e.g., music engineering technology, media writing and production, studio jazz writing, and keyboard performance and pedagogy. The project paper requires the student to document and communicate the purpose, nature, and outcomes of the culminating experience for students in these programs. The nature and scope of a project may vary considerably from one program to another.

A *doctoral essay* is usually the required document for doctoral students in a Doctor of Musical Arts (D.M.A.) program in performance or composition. Much of the distinction between a *doctoral essay* and a *doctoral dissertation* is a matter of usage, with the essay being associated with the D.M.A. degree and the dissertation with the Doctor of Philosophy (Ph.D.) degree. A Ph.D. traditionally is considered a "research-oriented" academic degree. According to *Webster's Third International Dictionary* (1971, 656), the dissertation associated with the degree typically is based on independent research and should provide evidence of the candidate's mastery of both subject matter and scholarly method.

In contrast, a D.M.A. degree is considered an "applied" or professional degree, and the essay associated with it usually is of an analytic, interpretive, or critical nature and may be somewhat shorter, less systematic, and less formal than a dissertation. Nevertheless, "it [the essay] must present evidence of a thorough acquaintance with some limited special field, obtained by recourse to original sources" (777).

In some instances, a doctoral essay in music serves a function similar to the recital paper for the master's student in a performance program: It allows a student to document the analysis, study, preparation, and pedagogy of works performed on a major culminating recital, with the primary difference between the master's paper and the doctoral essay being a matter of scope and depth. Other doctoral essays, however, may examine the works of a given composer for a particular performing medium, study developments in performance practices, or focus on the pedagogical aspects of selected repertoire. Central to most doctoral essays is documentation of analytic, descriptive, and/or interpretive examination of a substantial body of music from the perspective of a performer, conductor, or composer. Students usually earn from 12 to 18 credits for a doctoral essay.

A *doctoral dissertation* is usually the culminating written work for Ph.D. students in musicology, music theory, and music education. A Ph.D. is considered a research-oriented degree, and the credit allotment for the Ph.D. dissertation usually ranges from 15 to 24 credits. The research methodology may vary considerably both across and within disciplines, but a majority of these studies involve the collection, analysis, and interpretation of original data. Others may involve the development and evaluation of music curricula and/or measurement and evaluation tools.

Regardless of the degree program or what the culminating paper is called, graduate students must be able to (a) describe and document the nature of their research, recital, or project and (b) communicate it clearly and effectively. Clear and effective communication is an essential aspect of graduate education, and the guidelines offered here, while not focused on writing per se, are believed useful in facilitating the clarity of communication in graduate music students' formal papers.

The Role of Scholarship in a Graduate Music Program

It is not uncommon for a student to be matriculated in a university graduate program and to have given little consideration to the purpose of the university in which they are enrolled; their considerable mental energies more often are directed toward the immediate goal of completing the education they seek. The authors believe it important to provide students with a modicum of understanding regarding the purpose of the educational enterprise in which they are involved so that the efforts expended in the process will also have some degree of meaning beyond the diploma and whatever opportunities it may afford.

Information and Ideas

In searching out the purpose of a university one must first consider the essence of a university. A university is more than the students, faculty, administration, buildings, print and electronic media, or any other physical entity. While these are critical components of a university, their presence alone does not constitute the true essence of a university. The authors submit that the essence of any university is, and should always remain, an open and inviting environment for the production, nurturing, and dissemination of ideas. It is crucial here to separate the concept of *information* from that of *ideas*. While information may be an abundant and seemingly valuable commodity, hence the oft cited usage of the term "information age" to describe the post-industrial period, information is little more than a necessary prerequisite for ideas. Information in the absence of ideas is analogous to having an elegant and efficient transportation system for which there is no destination. Ideas give action, direction, and purpose to information. Furthermore, ideas may be combined to form theories, provide explanations, describe phenomena, or predict outcomes.

Information differs from ideas in yet other ways. Information is often temporally limited to its state of currency, i.e., new information is constantly being generated and, consequently, previous information becomes outdated. Ideas are bound by neither time nor space, but rather by the limits of imagination and origination. Ideas and information together provide the basis of a body of knowledge, and it is to this corpus that universities contribute.

Scholarship

Not all ideas, however, are of equal merit. Competing, even contradictory, ideas must be scrutinized and adjudged worthy of retention. The uncritical acceptance of any idea can result in the perpetuation of myth and may diminish the integrity and purpose of the university or an entire body of knowledge. The process that has evolved to protect the integrity of a university and concomitantly to contribute to a body of knowledge has come to be referred to as *scholarship*. Scholarship is, essentially, the systematic collection and assessment of information for the purpose of the selection of critically examined tentatives with the goal of creating, validating, or refuting ideas. In the discipline of music, these ideas may be related to performance practice, pedagogical propositions, historical acumen, theoretical insights, or may be of a purely musical nature as occurs in the field of composition. True scholarship, moreover, extends beyond the generation and critical examination of ideas. As is consistent with the essence of a university, scholarship also implies the dissemination of ideas. Scholarship must be *shared* with others; the ideas must be reported so that others can examine, scrutinize, criticize, and, ultimately, learn from them. This is the basic nature of scholarship, and it is why there is a required scholarly component for advanced degrees in all universities.

Graduate Students as Scholars

When a student undertakes an advanced academic degree, the student assumes and accepts the responsibility to contribute to a body of knowledge, i.e., to develop, examine, test, and submit his or her ideas to a community of scholars. This is a serious and onerous task. It is also a rewarding pursuit.

The novice scholar may find some of the practices and traditions regarding the process of scholarship to be daunting. It should be remembered, however, that such practices have evolved so that communication can take place among scholars and ideas can subsequently be examined and exchanged. For real communication of any sort to take place, there must be a shared knowledge of expression and meaning among those involved. The more precise the expression, the less likely that miscommunication will occur. Scholarly discourse requires that very precise expressions be communicated with great clarity. Therefore, the "rules" of communication in scholarship are often quite exacting. The subtleties of standard scholarly practice make it necessary for the student scholar to observe these practices so that the content of his or her ideas can be assessed by the community of scholars free of distractions due to poor or imprecise communication. It is with these considerations in mind that this manual was undertaken.

Accuracy, Authenticity, Simplicity, and Clarity.

The process of scholarship is based in questions and questioning and as such necessitates that many critical value decisions be exercised by the individual scholar. The essential values or qualities of scholarly communication can be summarized with four words: *Accuracy, authenticity, simplicity, and clarity*. Typically, a fifth value, *originality*, is also a component in all scholarship that does not involve dependence upon replication (i.e., experimental validation or confirmation).

Information and ideas presented to a community of scholars and, ideally, to the world must be *accurate*. For this value to be represented in a document, there must be evidence that the information presented therein is exact, precise, and correct. Great numbers of equally frustrating and frightening anecdotes exist to exemplify the failure of scholars to attend to the quality of accuracy. Misquotations, misattributions, incorrect or incomplete documentation, illegitimate data, and the like undermine the scholarly enterprise and call into question all of the ideas and information presented in a document. Dubious information gathered haphazardly can result in only spurious interpretations and implausible conclusions. Such is the antithesis of scholarship.

Authenticity is directly related to accuracy. Authenticity, like accuracy, applies to both the information gathered and the ideas presented. Attributions of content and ideas must be authentic because there must be absolute conformity to the truth in order to maintain the integrity of scholarly inquiry. The source, or sources, of the content presented in a scholarly document must be appropriately recognized. Authenticity has particular relevance for scholars who undertake historical research. Verification of sources of information is the bulwark upon which most historical research is based; consequently, information that is authentic resonates with greater authority.

Moreover, in any research methodology, there typically is a review of related literature. A review of related literature is highly dependent on the authenticity of the information therein. This helps to provide a method for others to "trace the steps" of the author and to make certain that the originator of an idea is properly identified. Another aspect of authenticity in scholarship concerns the manner in which the scholar conducts him- or herself during the course of researching a topic. It may be tempting, for example, for a novice scholar to merely "paraphrase" an existing review of literature rather than to conduct an in-depth study personally. As with a failure to conform to accuracy, the failure to authentically gather the appropriate information undermines the credibility of the entire paper and the author.

Clarity and *simplicity* apply to the presentation of ideas and information. These two words seem, at least at first notice, to be direct descriptions of essential qualities of all writing. However, experience has demonstrated to the authors that these qualities are often lacking in documents of graduate student scholars. It has often been noted that there is a significant difference between *being* scholarly and *sounding* scholarly. This difference is the clarity and simplicity of the scholar's communication of ideas. If the central purpose of scholarship is to create and share ideas with others, then clarity of expression is a critical asset. An important and powerful idea can be obfuscated, discounted, or, even worse, ignored if the quality of a scholar's expression is inferior to that of the idea being expressed. Presentation cannot take the place of substance in scholarship; however, in the absence of the former, the latter is severely compromised. The best writing is direct, active, and clear. It is a scholarly adage that if the author cannot state his or her ideas clearly and succinctly, he or she may not fully understand the topic being addressed.

However, it should also be recognized that scholars must moderate between the qualities of simple communication and precision in language. The English lexicon is vast and refined. Therefore, scholars should be exact, and exacting, in their expression. Words have *meanings*, often very explicit and precise. When it is necessary for clarity, the author must use the word with the most precise meaning, again, to avoid miscommunicating an idea. This is not to suggest that specific and precise word-choice be confused with the unnecessary use of jargon, neologisms, or other displays of pedantry.

Originality is another quality that is present in most types of scholarship. Originality in some respects is a balance to the qualities of clarity and simplicity. Related to both accuracy and authenticity, originality in the interpretation of existing information, development or application of a method of inquiry, or of an idea itself is the capstone of much scholarship. It might be said that the essence of scholarly originality is the ability of the scholar to observe what everyone else sees and to conclude that which no one else has. Many find this the most intimidating aspect of the scholarly endeavor. To be original is to be at risk, and risk is very uncomfortable. Originality requires one to be inventive, imaginative, and even oppositional. To fail to be original is not always a shortcoming in scholarship, but much scholarship that does not demonstrate originality is also unremarkable.

Selecting a Topic

The caustic reviewer who noted that a manuscript was "both good and original, but the part that was good was not original and the part that was original was not good" points out the importance of the essential qualities of scholarship. The statement also points to the fact that the competent scholar must go beyond the rigorous details of conformity to style and method. If scholarship is to have genuine value, it must be substantive, that is, worthy of undertaking. It is important to be able to say something well, but one must first *have* something to say. It is not uncommon for someone to utter the query "so what?" at the conclusion of a scholarly presentation. It is the responsibility of the scholar to make certain that there *is* an answer. While this manual is not intended to guide the scholar regarding the intellectual substance of a topic or the integrity of the endeavor, it is, rather, presented to facilitate those who have a desire to contribute to a body of knowledge and further advance the mission of all universities.

Selecting a topic can be a difficult first step in the process of scholarship. An initial point at which to begin is by conducting some basic library research to develop a working knowledge of available information and resources related to an area of study. This library research can assist the student in selecting, narrowing, revising, or rejecting a topic.

Strategies for Library Research

Before undertaking in-depth research on a potential topic, it is helpful for students to do preliminary reading in standard sources such as *The New Grove Dictionary of Music and Musicians* (Sadie 2001) and *The New Harvard Dictionary of Music* (Randel 1986) in order to become familiar with terms associated with a topic. It is also useful to examine the bibliography following an encyclopedia article to get a quick idea of the extent of the literature available on the topic and to note authors of previous books and articles who are considered experts in the field. One can use these terms and names as access points when searching on-line databases.

The key to library research lies in successful searching of a library's on-line catalog, which provides bibliographic and location information for books, music scores and recordings, videos, maps, government documents, microforms, computer software, and periodical titles. A library catalog will *not* include references to *articles* published in journals, magazines, or newspapers. To locate *articles,* one should consult general and subject databases, which will be discussed later.

Types of Searches

While not comprehensive, the following types of searches are characteristic of most on-line library catalogs. Examples will illustrate when a certain type of search would yield the best results. A *keyword* search is used when the researcher does not know an exact title or subject or when two or more concepts are combined (e.g., *piano music* [and] *black composers*). This is the broadest search because it checks terms in the title, subject, and content fields. One should use a keyword to search for a song title on a recording or in a collection (e.g., *Moon over Miami*).

A *subject* search begins with a term from a controlled vocabulary (Library of Congress Subject Headings) that is assigned by librarians. A good strategy is to search for a title obtained from the bibliography of an encyclopedia article and to note the subject heading found towards the end of the bibliographic record; this subject heading can then be used to search for further titles. Subject searches are more specific than keyword searches (e.g., *Internet resources).*

A *title* search may be used when the exact title or the first few words of the title are known (e.g., *Traviata*).

Author searches are used to locate works by a specific author or organization. For music, authors include composers of musical works and performers on sound recordings or videos (e.g., *John Coltrane*). One may also use names of authors found in bibliographies of encyclopedia articles to do further searches on a specific topic.

A person can also *limit* a search by specifying a certain type of material (e.g., recordings), language of the material, or publication dates (e.g., search subject *Operas*, limit by material type *video*).

Sources for Books

After searching the local library catalog, one can search for books in other databases such as *WorldCat*, http://firstsearch.oclc.org/dbname=WorldCat; or commercial databases such as *Books in Print* or *amazon.com*. Searches are conducted using the same terms and strategies as in the local library catalog searches. Additional sources may be found by consulting the footnotes and bibliographies in books found on a topic. If the needed materials are not available in one's local library, it may be possible to borrow the book or journal through the library's interlibrary loan department. It should be noted that policies regarding the use of interlibrary loan vary from one library to another.

Sources for Articles

Three databases particularly useful for finding music articles are *RILM Abstracts*, http://firstsearch.oclc.org/dbname=RILM; *International Index to Music Periodicals, Full Text Edition*, http://iimpft.chadwyck.com/; and *Music Index Online*, http://www.hppmusicindex.com/out.asp. Most databases offer on-line help screens, as well as options for simple or advanced searches. One should always check the dates covered by the on-line databases. For older journal articles, it may be necessary to consult print indexes such as *Music Index*.

Certain general databases such as *Academic Search Elite* and *Article 1ˢᵗ* also contain music articles. Most library catalogs and web pages list the titles of databases the library receives on subscription. Some on-line sources require passwords; again, one should check the policies of the local library.

Dissertations

The most comprehensive source for dissertation titles is *Dissertation Abstracts*, which is available online http://firstsearch.oclc.org/dbname=Diss; a specific source title for musicology dissertations is *Doctoral Dissertations in Musicology*, by Cecil Adkins and Alis Dickinson. The print version is updated by DDM-online http://www.music.indiana.edu/ddm/.

Recordings

Recordings can be found in one's library catalog and also in *WorldCat*. The subject term *Discographies* should be used when searching for lists of recordings. Good sources for CDs are web sites such as http://www.allmusic.com or http://www.amazon.com. Other sources include the web sites of record publishers.

Scores

Music scores can be found through a library's on-line catalog and *WorldCat*. Many specialized bibliographies of music also exist, but there is no such thing as a comprehensive *Music in Print*. For on-line sources, one should also check web sites of individual music publishers.

Web Sources

Web sources can be found through internet search engines such as Google, Yahoo, or Alta Vista. Certain universities have compiled lists of links to music web pages. One exhaustive list is maintained by Indiana University:

http://www.music.indiana.edu/music_resources/ and another by
Harvard University:
http://hcl.harvard.edu/loebmusic/text/siteindex.html#research.

Limitations

Readers should be aware of the limited intent of the guidelines presented in this manual. They are intended to assist music
students with preparation of theses, essays, dissertations, and
other formal papers that might be required as part of a graduate
degree in music. Given this intent, the focus is on organization
and preparation of the paper. The manual does not address matters of writing style and grammar usage. Ideally, students already
will have developed adequate skills in writing and grammar usage
before pursuing graduate study. If one discovers after entering
graduate study that basic writing skills are lacking, he/she should
either take a basic course in technical writing or at least conduct
some self-study using one of the many available sources such as
Strunk and White's (1959) classic *The Elements of Style*,
Montgomery and Stratton's (1981) *The Writer's Hotline Handbook*,
William and Mary Morris' (1975) *Harper Dictionary of Contemporary
Usage, The Chicago Manual of Style* (1993), or Walters' (1999) *The
Readable Thesis: A Guide to Clear and Effective Writing,* which was
written specifically to facilitate writing in music students' graduate
theses and dissertations. The Turabian and APA style manuals
also offer excellent guidelines related to basic writing style and
grammar usage.

Students should take care to match their talents, tempera-
ments, and training in the selection of both a topic and an advisory committee. Interest in a topic and desire to complete a
degree alone cannot take the place of a certain level of expertise
and ability. While members of the advisory committee can aug-
ment or complement individual student abilities, such as providing guidance regarding statistical applications or interpretations,
students should not undertake research methodologies or pursue
studies that are beyond their abilities and coursework.

It is typically inappropriate for students to engage an outside consultant to assist them in the design and/or analysis of the data for a study that is to be a demonstration of the culmination of their coursework for a terminal degree. It is likewise inappropriate for students to engage an editor for the preparation of a typescript, as it is expected that knowledge of basic grammar, syntax, and orthography is prerequisite for entrance into any graduate program. This is a complicated issue, however, given that graduate programs across the United States are welcoming students from various cultures and ethnicities. Competence in written English expression remains a universal expectation in graduate programs in this country, and students should be fully aware of this expectation upon entrance. This caveat does not extend to students engaging a typist to assist with the preparation of a typescript or a consultant to assist with the preparation and presentation of musical examples or other figures in the text. Such technical assistance does not present the same potential for jeopardizing the integrity of the scholarly enterprise as do consultants who contribute substantively to a project.

❊ 2 ❊
Documentation Systems and Issues

Graduate students in music are expected to demonstrate both high level musicianship and scholarship. High level scholarship requires the ability to write in a scholarly manner. Notions regarding the nature of scholarly writing undoubtedly vary, but, as noted in Chapter 1, the essence of scholarly writing may be reduced to four essentials: accuracy, authenticity, simplicity, and clarity. Information and ideas must be accurate and authentic, and they must be presented simply and clearly.

Documentation is concerned with providing evidence that information and ideas presented in a paper are accurate and authentic. Authors who fail to document sources adequately do not meet these two important criteria for scholarly writing. In addition, the information and ideas must be comprehensible to a reader. Simplicity and clarity in writing are essential to making writing comprehensible. Thus, documentation must be as simple, straightforward, and clear as possible. To the extent that a graduate student can do this, his or her writing is scholarly.

Scholarly writing requires a clear system of documentation and application of the system in a consistent style. The intent of this chapter is to (a) provide an overview of two basic systems for documentation in writing, (b) examine some bases for selecting one or the other of the systems, and (c) provide an introduction to the two documentation systems as espoused by two of the most popular style manuals used by graduate students: *A Manual for Writers of Term Papers, Theses, and Dissertations* (Turabian 1996)[2] and the *Publication Manual of the American Psychological Association* (APA 2001). The chapter concludes with a brief discussion of

16

some ethical concerns related to academic writing. The information in the discussion of ethical concerns is drawn primarily from the APA manual (2001, 348-355).

Systems of Documentation

The traditional system of documentation used in graduate theses, essays, dissertations, and term papers is the *Footnote-Bibliography* system. Still the preferred system for writing in the humanities, particularly for historical inquiry, the system essentially involves providing, in a footnote, a specific reference to a source cited and including a reference to the source in a bibliography at the end of the paper. A variation of the footnote-bibliography systems is the *Endnote-Bibliography* system, which places the specific reference to a source at the end of a chapter rather than in a footnote.

The other basic system of documentation is the *Reference* system, which often is referred to as the *Author-Date* system. Essentially, this system involves including an author's surname and the date of a publication parenthetically in the text following the information, idea, or quotation for a source. If a source is quoted directly, the specific page number also must be included. A *Reference List* is included at the end of the paper. The reference list is an alphabetical list by author of all sources cited in the paper, and it usually differs from a bibliography in organization, format, and sources included.

Selecting a System

A university's graduate school may accept theses, essays, and dissertations using either system of documentation, but a writer must choose one system and use it consistently throughout a paper. However, the choice of a system may not always rest with the writer. Some departments and some professors expect their students to use a particular system. Traditionally, musicologists and others concerned with historical research insist that students use the footnote-bibliography system. Music educators and music therapists now use the reference system almost exclusively. Besides the traditions of a particular discipline, instructors of some courses may insist that all students use a particular system and even a specific style manual. The Turabian manual provides guidelines and examples for using either system; the APA manual provides guidelines and examples only for the author-date reference system. Should a department or professor require the use of a style manual other than Turabian or APA, they should provide students with guidelines and examples for documenting references to musical scores, notation, electronic sources, and so forth. Before beginning any writing project for a term paper, thesis, essay, dissertation, or other writing project, students should consult with the major professor involved to determine whether a particular system or style manual must be used. If none is specified, the selection of a system and style manual becomes a matter for the student to choose.

The recommendation here is for a student to confine his or her choice to one of the basic systems mentioned above; also, it is recommended that students limit their choice of style manual to either Turabian or APA. The use of Turabian or APA is important for music students, since the present manual provides guidelines for documenting music examples, recordings, and electronic sources in a manner that is consistent with the styles in which the Turabian and APA manuals document traditional printed sources.

Contemporary word processing systems such as Microsoft Word® and WordPerfect® have greatly reduced the typing and other mechanical problems related to the footnote-bibliography system. Numbering footnotes and spacing them on a page can now be done more-or-less automatically. Nevertheless, from a *writer's* perspective, the author-date reference system is much easier to use. However, many *readers*, especially graduate advisors, prefer to see the specific documentation for a source on the page on which it is cited; other advisors seem to be satisfied with the reference system. Besides an advisor's preference, there are two additional considerations when deciding whether to use or not use the footnote-bibliography system: (a) How important is it to have the specifics (i.e., the title of the source and the place of publication) on the same page as the reference to the source? and (b) How distracting will the footnotes on a page be to a reader? One occasionally reads papers in which many pages will have less than one-half page of text with the balance of these pages filled with footnotes. Also, the use of footnotes may lengthen a paper considerably. Unless the discipline, department, or advisor specifically requires that the footnote-bibliography system be used, the author-date reference system is recommended.

Selecting a Style Manual

Once the author makes the decision regarding the basic system of documentation, one must still decide which style manual to follow. If the footnote-bibliography system is used, the Turabian style manual is the only choice, since it provides guidelines and examples for documenting via the footnote-bibliography system. If the reference system is selected, one may choose between the Turabian and APA style manuals, and this is a difficult decision. Both are excellent style manuals, and differences in the difficulty of using them seem negligible. Besides information related to documentation, each style manual provides much useful information about (a) organization of a paper, including format, systems of headings, and major sections of a paper, (b) punctuation and capitalization, and (c) grammar, language usage, and writing styles.

Both style manuals are designed to serve more than one purpose. For example, the Turabian manual provides guidelines and examples for writing term papers, theses, essays, and dissertations in either the footnote-bibliography system or the reference system. A user of the manual must be careful to distinguish between examples for the two systems of documentation.

The APA manual is "intended primarily as a guide to preparing manuscripts for journal publication" (APA 2001, 321), but it also provides guidelines for writing theses, dissertations, and other student papers. A student using the APA manual for student papers must adhere closely to the guidelines of the manual's Chapter Six, which provides general organizational and format guidelines for papers not being submitted for publication.

Several additional factors may have a bearing on which manual to select. One's previous experience with a given style manual may influence this decision, but other factors should be considered. For example, does one have aspirations to write for publication beyond the thesis, essay, or dissertation? If so, one should consider the APA manual, since its focus is on preparing articles for submission to journals. The Turabian manual focuses primarily on writing term papers, theses, etc.

One also should examine several journals in one's discipline and note the style used. If most journals in a discipline use a particular style, it seems logical for a student to learn to use that style. The nature of the content of one's discipline also could influence the selection of a style manual. For example, if statistical data and tables will be a major part of one's paper, the APA manual may be the more appropriate style manual, because it offers more information than the Turabian manual regarding the reporting of statistical data and tables.

The Turabian manual appears to be used in more areas of academia than the APA manual, but the latter seems to have some particular advantages. Nevertheless, the choice between the two style manuals usually remains with the student, and the present manual was designed to accommodate either.

Some Ethical Concerns

Regardless of the documentation system or style manual used, student writing must meet certain ethical principles that underlie all scholarly writing. While these principles are implicit in this handbook's essentials of scholarly writing (accuracy and authenticity), it may be useful to discuss them a bit further here. According to the APA manual, the ethical principles that underlie scholarly writing are designed to "ensure the accuracy of scientific and scholarly knowledge and . . . to protect intellectual property rights" (348). The principles relate specifically to (a) reporting of results, (b) plagiarism, (c) publication credit, (d) duplicate publication of data, (e) sharing data, and (f) reviewers' responsibilities.

Regardless of the nature of the scholarly inquiry—whether philosophical, descriptive, historical, or experimental research; bibliographical or other library research; or musical analysis and description—the results must reflect a level of integrity that is beyond reproach. Results must clearly be based on the findings of the scholarly inquiry, including those that may not necessarily support one's research hypothesis, and be reported as honestly and accurately as possible.

Issues of plagiarism are particularly troublesome. Information or ideas drawn from someone else's work must be acknowledged, even if they are paraphrased rather than quoted. As stated in the APA manual (349), "the key element of this principle is that an author does not present the work of another as if it were his or her own work. This can extend to ideas as well as written words." The reference system of documentation allows writers to easily acknowledge sources of knowledge and ideas without interrupting the flow of the text.

Publication credit is less a concern for student papers than for typescripts submitted for publication. However, when group projects or other research efforts involve several students, all persons contributing to the writing and/or making substantial contributions to a study should receive authorship credit; persons making obviously lesser contributions may simply be acknowledged in a footnote. Special issues may arise when students and faculty collaborate on a project. In some instances the student may be the primary investigator, but often the contributions of the faculty member are essential for designing, carrying out, and/or analyzing data from a study. Any subsequent publication of a study involving co-authorship between students and faculty must include as authors only those who have contributed substantially to the study. Advisors, committee members, and department chairs should not automatically be credited as co-authors in the publication of a student's work.

While issues related to duplicate publication of data are a major concern in journal articles, such issues also are an ethical concern in student papers. It is unethical to submit articles based on the same data to more than one journal; neither should the same typescript be submitted to more than one journal at the same time.

Similarly, students should not submit essentially the same term paper for more than one course. The primary point of scholarly inquiry is to gain knowledge, and a student who fails to conduct independent research for different courses borders on cheating both themselves and the integrity of the academic endeavor. This is not to imply that a research theme or series of studies related to a broad topic is completely unethical; developing a series of studies or approaching a broad topic from different perspectives often is necessary and desirable. A student must, however, ensure that each study is indeed an independent study, adding some new dimension to the research theme or direction.

Scholarly inquiry should be subject to verification, and specific research procedures should be clearly defined so that others may replicate a study. If others question one's data analysis, a researcher should make the data available for others to analyze. This often is easily accomplished by including raw data and other relevant documents in an appendix to a study. Obviously, the confidentiality of any subjects participating in a study must be maintained, and any cost involved in sharing data should be borne by the requester. Data from a study should be retained for a minimum of five years (APA, 354).

Editorial review committees for journals necessarily involve some circulation and discussion of a manuscript, but editors and reviewers "may not, without the author's explicit permission, quote from a manuscript or circulate copies for any purpose other than that of editorial review" (APA, 354-355). Within the confines of academia, students may expect that faculty advisors and committee members will function in a manner similar to an editorial review committee. Any use of a student's work by a faculty member must meet the same ethical standards that the profession holds for editorial review committees.

❋ 3 ❋
The Proposal Process

Introduction

The proposal for the culminating paper for a music degree program is a formal document that essentially serves as an implied contract between the student and the advisory committee. The proposal stipulates the conditions that the student must fulfill in the completed document. Therefore, the proposal is crucial to the successful completion of the final paper and as such is equally crucial to the successful completion of the degree program in which the student is enrolled. Since the proposal is a formal document, it must conform to the style manual to be used (see Chapter 2, page 17, Selecting a System) and should have the appropriate frontispieces (see Appendix C, Sample Frontispieces). These include a cover or title page, a signature page, an abstract, and a table of contents. The proposal should also include a bibliography or reference list. Upon completion, the formal proposal is submitted to, reviewed by, and defended before the complete advisory committee. This process of review and defense is referred to as the *proposal process*. Details of the proposal process may vary slightly due to the constitution of a particular committee, the nature of the proposed topic, and the dynamics of the process itself. The balance of this discussion provides general guidelines for the proposal process.

Purpose of the Proposal

A well-developed proposal provides the student, the advisor, and the advisory committee a common basis for communication regarding the project. This common basis includes detailed specifics regarding what the student intends to do, why the proposed project should be conducted, and how the student proposes to accomplish the project. The greater the detail and clarity of the proposal, the less likely that miscommunication will occur as the project progresses. While it is not uncommon that minor rethinking of some aspect of a project may occur during the process of developing the final paper, major disagreements regarding the nature of the proposed project can be avoided through careful adherence to the proposal process. In many instances, the proposal represents the initial chapters of the final document with only minor changes in tense (i.e., the proposal indicates what the student *will do* during the course of the project, and the final document serves as reportage of what *was done*). It is important for the student and the advisory committee to recognize that the proposal will become a substantial segment of the final document and therefore merits the same careful consideration to content, format, and presentation that is required in a final document. Upon completion of a formal proposal, a student defends his/her proposed project before the full advisory committee. Only after approval by the advisory committee may the student undertake the proposed project.

If the expectations regarding the project are made and communicated with specificity and clarity in the proposal and the student has the ability and determination to complete the document, the final defense of the completed project is typically a positive experience for all involved. The final defense provides a formal opportunity for the student to present the completed document and for the advisory committee to determine whether the completed document fulfills the covenant of the proposal.

Proposal Content

Following is a general outline for a proposal:

Introduction and Background
Description of the Problem
What is the general issue?
Statement of the Purpose
Which specific aspect(s) of the problem will the paper address?
Review of Related Literature
What has been written regarding the topic or this type of inquiry?
Procedures or Methodology
What specifically will be done to accomplish the purpose?
What specific procedures will be used to complete the research?
What specific research tools will be employed?
What specific source materials will be consulted?
References

Obviously, the specific content of the proposal can be as varied as the topics and methodologies explored therein. For example, a proposal for a recital paper is largely determined by the selection of repertoire for a recital. Consequently, its focus is on the rationale for selection of the repertoire, the order in which the works will be performed, and the nature of the information (analysis, performance concerns, etc.) to be included in the paper. Because of the nature of recital papers, the specifics of proposals for them are not discussed here.[3] Similarly, some project papers in special programs such as media writing and jazz writing are repertoire driven; hence, proposals for such projects are not discussed here. Students developing projects in such areas should work closely with their advisor and advisory committee in writing the proposal for such projects.

However, proposals for composition projects at both the master's and doctoral levels somewhat differ from the general outline. In essence, such proposals provide a rationale for and description of the proposed composition, and they should provide specific information about the scope, concept, and instrumentation of the proposed project. In addition to objective description of relevant aspects of formal structure, pitch/harmonic resources, melody, rhythm, dynamics, orchestration, etc., composition students are encouraged to discuss philosophical and aesthetic issues related to their proposed composition. Finally, they should provide some indication of the student composer's related compositions, experience with similar projects, compositional influences beyond one's personal experiences, and the likelihood for completing the project within the proposed timeframe.

Proposals for other master's level papers such as theses in musicology, music theory, music education, music therapy, and music engineering technology usually involve some type of data gathering, thus allowing students in these majors to follow the general outline.

Because doctoral dissertations and doctoral essays other than compositions usually are more extensive in scope than master's theses and projects, the general outline presented here is intended to illustrate the nature of the material to be included in a doctoral proposal. However, it is believed that the model can easily be applied to master's-level theses and projects.

As suggested, a typical proposal for a doctoral essay or dissertation has essentially five major sections: introduction, purpose, review of related literature, procedures, and summary. Typically, three of the five—the Introduction and Background, the Review of Related Literature, the Procedures or Methodology—should be conceived as potential chapters in the final document. It is in these sections that the student specifies what he or she intends to do, why it should be done, what has been done previously related to the project, and how it will be done.

The process of the student developing a dissertation proposal is analogous to an attorney building a case. One must examine precedent, provide evidence, and establish a believable position regarding the topic selected. However, the process essentially cannot begin until a decision regarding the topic has been made.

While discussion of the process of selecting a topic is beyond the scope of this manual, it is suggested that the student begin as soon as possible within the degree program to read the literature related to the area that presents the most interest for the student or has the most relevance to the student's personal and professional goals. Interest alone, however, does not always provide sufficient cause for the selection of a topic. Readings supervised by the student's advisor often can provide a background to determine if the topic will be a contribution to the body of knowledge. During this initial stage, the student should document the sources read by developing an annotated bibliography that can be useful in later stages of the dissertation process. There is no substitute for extensive readings in an area, and locating important information later is much easier when specific information regarding the source is readily available to the student.

A brief annotation for each entry usually is sufficient for recalling the importance of the source in question. The student should, however, make certain that the information in the annotation includes adequate detail so that he or she can clearly understand the annotation months or even years after encountering the source. Many institutions offer courses in music bibliography, and such courses provide an excellent opportunity for the student to develop an annotated list of sources to be consulted later. Readings can also provide the student with a working knowledge of the terminology, relevant keywords, authors, and style of scholarly writing regarding a particular topic. This is an indispensable but often overlooked part of the process of developing a research proposal. These comments regarding the selection of a topic are quite general; however, the specific suggestions for strategies for undertaking library research provided in Chapter 1 should be helpful to the process.

It is important to remember that a topic need not be totally novel to be appropriate as the subject for a thesis, essay, or dissertation. The lack of other writings in the area does not, in and of itself, signify that a topic is worthy of selection for a major scholarly work. On the other hand, if a topic has been thoroughly and *satisfactorily* examined in the literature, there is little reason for the student to undertake an examination of the topic. Unless the student can provide a unique, original, oppositional, or enhanced perspective on the topic, i.e., unless he or she has the potential to make a *contribution* to the body of knowledge, the search for a suitable topic should continue. Lastly, one should remember that a topic must be appropriate in terms of the total scope of the potential study and with respect to the individual student's available resources. If a topic is too broad and/or ill-defined, the student may not be able to bring the study to conclusion in a reasonable amount of time. If the topic is too narrow, there may be too little of substance about which to write. In any case, the student must always keep in mind that typically the process of scholarship is incremental in nature and that genuine growth within a body of knowledge is achieved through many small, interdependent steps rather than huge leaps. In summary, the decision regarding the selection of an appropriate topic should be thought through carefully with the aid and advice of the student's primary advisor. Working closely with one's advisor while selecting a research topic will do much to alleviate time spent in researching an area that might not contribute positively to the academic progress of the student and to a relevant body of knowledge. Once the topic is selected, the proposal process can move forward.

Initially, the proposal document will have an introduction wherein the student introduces and describes the "problem" or the general topic to be explored. This serves to orient the reader to the topic. The description of the general topic or problem should lead the reader to the specific purpose of the proposed study. The Introduction may also be conceived as providing a rationale for the proposed study. The building of this rationale may be thought of as analogous to an attorney providing the opening remarks at the beginning of a trial. During opening remarks, the attorney presents the major arguments or points of his or her case, but the details of the arguments are introduced later as testimony and other evidence. So it is with the Introduction section of the proposal. The Introduction may require the citation and/or summary of the opinions and findings of other scholars regarding the topic as part of the development of the rationale for the study. However, the Introduction generally does not present a full exploration of the related issues and literature. The detailed "evidence" that a scholar provides regarding the topic generally is reserved for the Review of Related Literature. Some scholars may find the distinction between the Introduction and the Review of Related Literature difficult to define, because the content of each may "overlap." The process of determining how much detail is required in the development of the rationale is best left to the student and his or her major advisor.

The Review of Related Literature should further support the argument that the research is worthy of undertaking. This might allay any concerns about the feasibility of the study based on what has already been written about the topic. Oftentimes the review will reveal insights regarding possible methodologies as well as additional topically related materials. It is important that the critical words in the title of this chapter be carefully considered. First, the chapter is a *review*, i.e., the literature is to be summarized, analyzed, and, where appropriate, critiqued so that a clear connection to the proposed project can be demonstrated. Second, *related literature* should include *relevant* research or other writings, including those from other fields that have implications for the proposed study. For example, performance anxiety is of concern to performers other than musicians, and learning strategies from other subject domains may have implications for pedagogy and learning in music. Finally, the judicious use of subheadings to group together related topics, studies, or ideas can help a reader follow the logic of the student in developing the proposal.

The first two chapters should convince the reader that the study is important and worthy of undertaking. The third chapter, usually entitled Procedures or Methodology, should assure the reader that the student is capable of completing the tasks before him or her. This requires clear specification of the procedures by which the study's purpose will be accomplished. If the study is historical in nature, the specific source materials, both primary and secondary, should be carefully described, including how they will contribute to fulfilling the study's purpose. In an experimental study, the research design, the evaluative tools, and data analysis procedures must be thoroughly and clearly discussed. In short, whatever research methodology is employed, the procedures for conducting the study must be clearly described. It also is important to specify a timeline for completion of the project.

The Proposal Process

The proposal process for students completing the D.M.A. degree program and those completing the Ph.D. differ only slightly.

Doctoral Essay Proposal

The process may vary from one university to another, but ordinarily the formal proposal for the doctoral essay is not submitted and defended until after the satisfactory completion of the qualifying recital, the initial doctoral recital, the selected tool subjects, and the doctoral qualifying examination. The selection of the proposal topic and the development of the formal proposal are a shared responsibility of the student, the student's advisor, and the other members of the doctoral committee. Following the submission of the proposal to the advisory committee for review, the student must schedule a date for a formal defense of the proposal. Again, procedures for scheduling a defense vary, but students must plan to allow each member of the doctoral committee to have a copy of the completed proposal for review at least two weeks prior to the date set for the defense.

Doctoral Dissertation Proposal

Following the satisfactory completion of the doctoral qualifying examination, the selected tool subjects, and the comprehensive examination, the student should develop, submit, and defend a formal proposal for the doctoral dissertation to the doctoral committee. The selection of the proposal topic and the development of the formal proposal are a shared responsibility of the student, the student's advisor, and the other members of the doctoral committee. Following the submission of the proposal to the committee for their review, the student must schedule a date for a formal defense, following the same procedures as for doctoral essay proposals. Students must plan to allow each member of the doctoral committee to have a copy of the completed proposal for review at least two weeks prior to the date set for the defense.

Communicating with Your Advisory Committee

The process of developing a proposal demands the involvement of the student, the student's advisor, and the student's committee. How each of these constituents participates may vary considerably from situation to situation. The particular dynamics of the process is largely determined by those involved. However, as soon as the committee is selected, it is advisable that the student assumes the responsibility for keeping each member of the committee informed as the project develops. Providing periodic written updates to each committee member should minimize misunderstandings regarding the project. It also is advisable to develop a timeline for the project in cooperation with the committee so that all involved are informed of deadlines and other relevant considerations.

❉ 4 ❉
Master of Music Recital Papers

R*ecital papers* are typically required for degrees in the performance areas, while *theses* usually are the culminating documents
for degrees in music education, music therapy, music theory, and
musicology. Because master's recital papers typically differ considerably from theses, the authors believe they warrant a separate
discussion. Therefore, this chapter will address matters related to
the development, submission, defense, and approval of a Master
of Music recital paper.

A particular concern related to the preparation of recital
papers is the timing of the writing and defense of the paper.
Higher education is replete with graduate students who have completed all requirements for a degree except the final paper.
Obviously, culminating papers for a degree will come toward the
end of a degree program, but in the case of recital papers, it is
believed to be in the best interest of the student if the paper is
completed and defended prior to the recital. The purpose of a
recital paper is to help the student recitalist gain an in-depth
understanding of the historical, analytical, and performance
aspects of the music to be performed. Such understanding
should greatly enhance the preparation of the recital. Policies will
vary from one university to another regarding the timing of the
writing and defense of a recital paper, but the authors believe that
a paper prepared post-recital is of no benefit in facilitating a student's performance of a recital.[4]

Content and Organization of Recital Papers

The subject of a recital paper is determined by the repertoire
to be performed during the recital. Typically, the paper will be

organized into chapters with the first chapter being the introduction and each subsequent chapter being devoted to a single selection. In some instances, such as a voice recital where several short songs or arias may be grouped together in some logical and meaningful fashion, the student may wish to address several selections collectively within a single chapter. Sometimes it may be appropriate to include a summary chapter following the chapters discussing the repertoire.[5]

It is not necessary to discuss each selection with the same focus or depth. Compositions of greater length, complexity, and/or historical importance may warrant greater discussion than compositions of lesser importance or of more conservative proportions. Also, discussions of the various selections may have different foci. For example, one selection may require discussion of issues related to the technical aspects of performance, while another may require more explanation related to its historical importance, and a third may require an extensive theoretical analysis.

Individual papers may also take on a particular focus, emphasizing one of the areas more so than the others. For example, some recital programs, and consequently the recital papers discussing the repertoire thereof, will demonstrate the historical development of a style, a genre, performance techniques, or even the instrument itself. Therefore, it is logical that such a recital paper focus on the historical elements the student wishes to emphasize as important. Other students may find that a chronological approach will help them better organize both the recital itself and the discussion of the important historical, theoretical, and performance ideas with respect to the recital repertoire. While recital program order is dictated by many factors, including mental or physical fatigue of the performer, the recital paper need not conform strictly to the order in which the selections were, or are to be, performed. Although it is not unusual that the chapters are organized in the order of presentation during the recital, other systems of organization are also possible. The student should recognize that the logical organization of the discussion of the repertoire in the recital paper sometimes requires a different sequence than the actual recital program.

It has been noted that "writing about music is like dancing about architecture," and as such, writing about music is admittedly a difficult task. This is especially true for students in applied music who have long focused their attention on technically polished performances of challenging repertoire. Having spent the majority of their efforts in "learning how to make music" rather than "learning about music" makes writing about music quite a demanding task for many performers. When developing the paper, it is often helpful for a student to keep a journal of problems, issues, discoveries, and other findings encountered while practicing and studying the music for the recital. Making marginal notes on the scores can also be very helpful to the student. Such notes can provide much material for the paper and will allow the student to gather the information over time rather than making the task so seemingly Herculean as when attempting to gather information all at one time. Moreover, when students keep notes about discoveries made regarding their repertoire, the information does not need to be "reconstructed" at a later date when recollection may not be so precise. Conscientious note taking can minimize frustration on the part of the student and make developing the paper a less arduous task.

While the specific content of each paper may vary for each individual recital program, the following suggestions are provided as guidelines. The Introduction is the one chapter in which the recital is discussed in its entirety, as subsequent chapters are focused on the individual selections. The Introduction should clearly state the purpose of the recital paper and introduce the recital repertoire in general terms. It should discuss how the paper will be organized, any focus or foci to be represented in the paper, and why and/or how the repertoire was selected; it should also explain how the repertoire represents a *recital* rather than just a collection of pieces performed at a single setting. Discussions of decisions regarding program order are also appropriate for inclusion in the Introduction. It is important for the student to recognize that a recital program is a planned event and not one that occurs as a result of the intervention of random chance. Emotional pacing, physical and technical limitations, historical concerns, and musical and aesthetic issues need to be considered when deciding program order. The process of making these decisions should be discussed in the Introduction. It is often helpful to discuss how the rest of the document is organized at the conclusion of the Introduction to serve as a transition to subsequent chapters. Each subsequent chapter will detail information regarding the historical, analytical, and performance issues that are of importance to the repertoire under discussion. While some "common thread" may weave the recital together, and this thread should be revealed in the paper, each chapter should essentially "stand alone." This means that each chapter should have a short introduction, a body that represents the three major areas of content, and some conclusion and/or summary. Appendix A provides a sample Introduction for a recital paper.

Issues of depth, breadth, and length often concern students while developing recital papers, but these factors will necessarily vary according to the nature and content of the recital repertoire. The student must be thorough and complete in informing the reader regarding the repertoire. It should be recognized that if there is very little to be written about a selection, one is left to ponder the worthiness of the selection for inclusion on an advanced performance degree recital program. Therefore, the student and the major advisor must plan carefully regarding the repertoire to be performed.

The following presents greater detail regarding the three primary topics to be discussed within the recital paper. These topics are historical information, theoretical information, and performance issues. In dealing with each of these topics in the recital paper the student is advised to remember that a certain degree of musical and scholarly sophistication exists on the part of the reader. However, the writer should provide clear explanations regarding any unique terminology, novel or unusual ideas, or subject-specific information to avoid confusion on the part of the reader. The student should consider how to make the description of the work as complete as possible by using these three perspectives. It is often helpful for the student to make observations from the differing perspectives that support each other; e.g., some historical event or information may be clarified by the theoretical analysis, which, in turn, enhances the performance of the work.

History

This section should orient the reader to the repertoire in terms of how the selection fits within the fabric of time. Detailed biographical information regarding well-known composers usually is not necessary. However, certain aspects of a famous composer's personal history may be important to include as they apply to the selection under discussion, e.g., if the work was influenced by a dramatic personal event of the composer's life, by a historical event such as a war or other political upheaval, or by a change in the composer's musical style due to the influence of other contemporaries. The student may find that lesser-known composers require more biographical information for the reader to better place the work within the general history of Western music, e.g., life dates, musical influences, education, and other significant background information that relates to the specific selection. Whatever information is included, the issues of authenticity and accuracy are of paramount importance.

Primary sources are generally preferred to secondary sources, and whenever possible confirmatory sources are recommended. The student must carefully observe the documentation of sources. In the recital paper, all sources used should be cited, and all sources cited should be used. Essentially, this means that the student is responsible for providing credit to the originator of an idea and that the bibliography should represent the resources used in developing the paper. This is little more than academic honesty, but the authors observe that students continue to demonstrate some difficulty with the concept.

When developing the important historical ideas in the recital paper, the student should always remember that the purpose of the paper is to provide greater insight regarding the music presented in the recital. If the student feels that the information is important to the understanding of the repertoire and may enhance the interpretation of the repertoire, then the information should be included. If the information does not meet this criterion, then the inclusion of the information is questionable.

Theoretical Analysis[6]

The discussion of the musical analysis of the repertoire is presented herein as a process with two stages. The first stage is the analysis that occurs before the writing of the document, and the second concerns the details of actually presenting the results of the analysis in the recital paper.

Initially, the student should examine the selection in terms of large organizational structures. The student should first attempt to discern the largest sections of a work or movement. Where appropriate, the student should examine thematic derivation, textural materials, and key relationships to ascertain a pattern in how the large sections work together as a musical process within the piece. Note should be made of how transitions between sections occur and how the composer deals with the issues of unity and variety. If the process conforms to a traditional intelligible form (e.g., sonata allegro, minuet and trio, rondo, etc.) such observations should be noted. It is also appropriate to examine a work for those characteristics that are unique or anomalous. These characteristics often create interpretive challenges to the performer and help to define the piece within the total available repertoire. These characteristics also provide the student with significant and interesting opportunities for discussion. When a piece conforms totally to expectations and traditions, there often is little for the student to discuss in the recital paper.

The pitch structure and the rhythmic structure of the piece should also be examined. If the selection is traditionally tonal, then the cadences and primary key areas of the large sections are important to locate. Sections that are departures from traditional expectations and those that present ambiguities are important and interesting should be noted for further discussion and commentary.

If the selection does not seem to conform to traditional tonal frameworks, the student needs to determine what pitch structures or pitch organization-schemas are used (e.g., modality, octatonic or other non-diatonic source scales, dodecaphonic serialism, free post-tonal relationships, random pitch-choice, microtonality, etc.). The student should attempt to make general observations regarding the overall pitch structure of the work under discussion, although it is not necessary to note those musical events that are not central to or remarkable within the piece. It is advisable for the student to remember that theoretical analysis should essentially be a systematic confirmation of what the ear has already revealed. This in mind, the student is cautioned to let the ear help in making decisions when analytical questions arise.

When presenting the results of the analysis in the recital paper the student should begin with a general statement of the overall formal structure of the selection or movement under consideration. It often is advisable to present a table or figure that summarizes the organization of the piece. Such an insert should be placed fairly early in the discussion of the selection and should amplify, clarify, or simplify the text of the analysis. Usually a phrasal analysis with measure number locations of major sections or major musical events, subsections, transitions, and principal key areas will suffice. Appendix H includes an example of such a table. It should be assumed that the interested reader has access to the complete score of the selection.

The text of the analysis section should lead the reader through the musical events summarized in the table, dealing with the large sections first, then moving through each work or movement in chronological sequence. While identification of major musical events within a piece is important, the analysis should be more than just a report of musical events. The student should seek to provide explanations for and insights into the musical processes and patterns present in the work. Making connections between the expressive effect of the discernible structures in a work and plausible explanations for *why* something occurs makes for a more interesting analysis than mere description of *what* occurs. The judicious use of musical examples (e.g., to demonstrate main themes or certain musical complexities) can enhance the text and are very illustrative. However, the student should remember that it is assumed that the reader has access to the complete score of the selection to which to refer if needed. When musical examples are inserted into the text, such insertions should occur at the conclusion of a paragraph rather than forcing a break in the text within a paragraph.

Generally, the student must guard against including too much detail about musical minutiae. The text should provide insight into the structure of the work under discussion and should be written as a guide for a competent musician to an unfamiliar work.

Performance Issues

This is arguably the most difficult section for most students to prepare. However, this section can and should serve as a culmination of the collective musical experiences and training received during the degree program. Students may include suggestions for practice strategies, performance considerations from both the performer's and the audience perspective, aesthetic considerations, specific technical challenges and/or observations (including, where appropriate, issues of ensemble), information about how each piece was approached with regard to presentation, and how some of the musical and technical problems posed by the work (and presented in the theoretical analysis) were approached and solved. This section often is highly personal and deals with individual perspective; however, for the sake of continuity within the document and for retaining the scholarly "tone" of the document, students should avoid using first person.

Committee Selection and Contributions

Recital papers, as with all formal scholarly documents submitted in partial fulfillment of degree requirements, are products that represent the academic integrity of the student, the faculty, and the institution granting the degree. As such, the committee shares in the responsibility for the development of the paper through the support each member provides to the student from the inception of the topic through the final defense of the recital paper. The selection of a committee is an important aspect of the process of developing a successful recital paper. Typically, the student's major professor serves as the Chair of the Committee. Selections of the remainder of the committee should be made in consultation and with the approval of the Committee Chair. When selecting members of the committee, students should be mindful of the contribution each member will make to the final paper.

While each institution has specific guidelines regarding graduate committee membership (e.g., no less than three members total, one of whom must be a member of the graduate faculty, and one member must be outside of the department in which the degree is being offered), additional considerations are important as well. The committee members should be able to provide guidance regarding the three aspects of the repertoire to be discussed in the recital paper (i.e., historical, analytical, and performance and/or pedagogical issues). Therefore, the members of the committee should be able to complement each other in terms of their expertise in these areas. The student's major professor should provide guidance as to who among the faculty the student may wish to have on the committee and who has the expertise to enhance the quality of the document.

Recital papers submitted in partial fulfillment of the requirements of performance degrees may not require the submission of formal proposals; however, students should make certain that the repertoire selected for the recital meets with the approval of the student's major advisor and, in the best of cases, the members of the committee. Communication with and among the members of the committee is largely the responsibility of the individual student. Establishing how the members of the committee wish to work with the student on the paper early in process can minimize misunderstandings at a more critical juncture. The student should inquire how each member wishes to be informed of the progress of the paper (e.g., chapter-by-chapter or as a finished project) and then comply with the wishes of the members. Typically, it is the student's responsibility to schedule and confirm any and all meetings of the committee, including the final defense. The student should also carefully adhere to all institutional deadlines and guidelines.

❊ 5 ❊
Format Issues

Most graduate papers are expected to meet some basic formatting standards. Besides such practical matters as allowing space for binding and enhancing the readability and organization of a paper, details of format often influences a reader's first impression of the content of the paper. If the format of a paper is clear, consistent, and reflects careful organization, many readers will make the assumption that the writer was also careful in researching and writing about the topic. Conversely, if the format of a paper is inconsistent, sloppy, and reflects little attention to details of format, a reader might infer that the quality and content of the information presented in the paper also are lacking. Obviously, careful attention to format is no substitute for weaknesses in research, inadequate knowledge of subject matter, and lack of clear and lucid writing; on the other hand, lack of attention to matters of format may lead advisors and other readers to read the content of a paper even more critically than they might otherwise. Also, and perhaps even more important, graduate students should make every effort to present the highest quality work possible in their academic writing. Appropriate format is one aspect of quality in academic writing.

This chapter provides some guidelines for enhancing the format of a graduate research paper. If one's university or academic program has other specific guidelines, they should take precedence over these. In the absence of specific guidelines, however, the ones offered here should be useful.

General Format Issues

This section provides guidelines for formatting a paper. The discussion assumes that most student papers are now typed on word processors rather than typewriters and that the student writer has at least basic knowledge of the particular word processor being used.

Setting the layout of the page before beginning to type will alleviate many subsequent problems in formatting and writing a paper. Basic layout parameters include font selection, margin and justification settings, line spacing, and page number placement.

The recommended font is *Times*, which may have various names on different word processors. Two *Times* fonts, *CG Times* and *Times New Roman*, are available in Microsoft® Word and WordPerfect®, two of the most popular word processors. Either is acceptable. The preferred font size is 12, and it should be used throughout the paper. With few exceptions, regular fonts should be used throughout the paper. Exceptions might include the use of **bold** or ***bold italics*** for headings and the use of *italics* for foreign terms, titles of major musical works, and titles of books and journals. Common Italian musical terms generally are not italicized. If using *italics*, one should avoid the use of underlining, which was used to indicate *italics* when typing on a typewriter. Also, one should be judicious in using quotation marks to emphasize words or phrases.

Margin settings should be consistent throughout the entire paper, and papers should be left-justified only. The standard page layout is to have one-inch margins at the top, bottom, and right-hand side of each page and a left-hand margin of one and one-half inches. The first page of the paper, however, begins two inches below the top of the page, and if the paper is divided into chapters, the first page of each chapter also should have a two-inch margin at the top of the page. Other major sections of a paper such as the Table of Contents, References, and Appendixes also should have a two-inch margin at the top of the first page.

It is recommended that each chapter of a paper be kept in a separate *File* in the word processing program being used to prepare the typescript. This greatly facilitates editing and revising. Once the paper is complete and ready for pagination as a whole, one simply repaginates each chapter by indicating *start at page number* (of the page following the last page number of the preceding chapter) instead of beginning each chapter with page number 1.[7]

All headings should be in boldface. The major heading for each chapter of a paper should be centered, in all capital letters (all caps) two inches below the top edge of the paper. A *centered* heading is centered between the margins, not the edges of the paper. To ensure a two-inch margin from the top of the first page (and the first page of each chapter if the paper is so divided), one simply begins on the fifth line, or two double spaces, below the one-inch margin that has been set for the entire paper (or chapter). If a paper is *not* divided into chapters, the title of the paper should be used as the heading for the major body of the paper. If a paper is divided into chapters, the chapter number, as shown at the beginning of each chapter in this manual, should be the first line of the page and be followed by the chapter title in all caps on the second line, or one double space, below the chapter number. Chapter numbers should be in Arabic numerals.[8]

The text of the chapter begins on the third line below the chapter title, leaving two blank spaces between the chapter title and the first line of the text. An introductory paragraph usually precedes the first subheading of a chapter; however, there may be instances when one chooses to omit an introductory paragraph. In such instances, the first subheading begins on the third line below the chapter title. All subsequent headings, which also are in boldface type, are simply double-spaced. Appendix B provides a sample system of headings.

Setting the page numbering system before beginning to type also is very helpful. Page numbers on the first page of each chapter should be placed at the bottom center of the page. Subsequent pages of each chapter should be numbered in the upper right-hand corner of the page and aligned with the top and right margins. The effect of this is that the first line of text for each page numbered in the upper right-hand corner actually begins one inch plus a double space below the top edge of the page. Assuming the paper is typed on a word processor, the procedure for doing this should be learned as one learns to use the word processor. Also, the page numbers must be of the same font type and size as the text.

Formatting Frontispieces

Sometimes general format issues seem minor in comparison to the problems encountered when formatting frontispieces. Many university graduate offices provide a particular format to be used for title pages and signatory pages, thus avoiding the problem. If not, the student needs to include the relevant information in an appropriate format.

Relevant information for a title page usually includes the following: (a) the name of the university, (b) the title of the paper, (c) the author, (d) the type of paper, e.g., master's thesis, doctoral essay, or doctoral dissertation, (e) to whom and for what purpose the paper is being submitted, (e) the city and state, and (f) the date of graduation. Appendix C provides sample title pages for a master's recital paper and a doctoral essay or dissertation and a sample signatory page for a doctoral essay or dissertation. Space markings are included on the samples to facilitate typing. Care should be taken to maintain the same margins for the frontispieces as for the paper proper; i.e., the information must be centered between the one and one-half inch margin on the left and one-inch margin on the right.

Preparing a Table of Contents also tends to be troublesome. Some word processing programs will do some of this automatically if a person can use the word processing program to its full capacity. In the authors' experience, however, graduate students in music usually cannot.

A Table of Contents must list the chapter titles and all subheadings for each chapter. It does not need to include any frontispieces that *precede* it, but it should include any frontispieces that follow it (e.g., List of Musical Examples), all chapter titles and subheadings, references (or bibliography), and each appendix. Each appendix usually has a title page.

The mechanical aspects of preparing a Table of Contents obviously will vary from one word processing program to another, but a sample by-the-numbers procedure for setting up the format for one in Microsoft® Word is shown in Appendix D. This particular format allows for three levels of headings. Use of capitalization within a Table of Contents should appear exactly as in the headings within the paper proper. Again, one should be sure to maintain the same margins as for the paper proper.

The basic procedures for setting up a List of Musical Examples, List of Tables, or List of Figures are essentially the same as for setting up the Table of Contents. Care should be taken to list the number of the example, table, or figure, the exact caption, and the page number.

Special Format Issues for Music Papers

The basic format described above is useful for most parts of most papers about music, but several additional problems exist for persons writing about music. Three particular problems, the formatting of reference, footnote, and/or bibliographical entries, the use of simple notation in the text, and the preparation and inclusion of musical examples, tables, and figures, warrant extended discussion and are discussed in subsequent chapters of this manual. Other format problems encountered when writing about music include the use of foreign terminology, references to musical genres and titles of musical works, and inclusion of musical scores and lead sheets.

Should all musical terminology that is considered *foreign* be italicized? Helm and Luper (1982, 70-71) note that in recent American usage foreign terms are being italicized less frequently. They suggest italicizing a word only if readers are likely to be unfamiliar with it. If an unfamiliar foreign word is to be used frequently throughout a paper, however, they suggest italicizing it only the first time it appears. Helm and Luper's recommendation appears to be a useful guideline, but it does require a writer to make an assessment of the readership's level of understanding of the terminology used.

Helm and Luper (1982, 71) also provide useful guidelines for citing musical works in the text. They recommend italicizing large works such as Mozart's *Symphony No. 40 in G Minor, K. 550* or Beethoven's *String Trio in E-flat Major, Op. 3.* References to genres such as symphonies, concerti, and overtures or to an individual work that is not the full exact title of a large work should be neither italicized nor capitalized, thus, Beethoven's first symphony or Mozart's clarinet concerto.

Helm and Luper recommend that titles of unpublished or small works be placed within quotation marks. Titles of songs or movements within multi-movement works also should be placed within quotation marks. However, this raises the question, What should be done when discussing a movement of a work that is called *Andante Cantábile*? It usually would be italicized because it is a foreign language, but should it be *"Andante Cantábile"*? Or *Andante Cantábile*? Or "Andante Cantábile"? Obviously a writer must make a decision and follow it consistently. Ordinarily quotation marks would be used around the italicized words, unless one considers the term sufficiently Americanized to omit the italics, in which case one would write "Andante Cantábile." The important point is to be consistent in format just as one must be consistent in matters of style and usage.

The inclusion of scores and lead sheets in an appendix is necessary for many music papers, particularly those involving original compositions or arrangements. Most scores and lead sheets are prepared without consideration of the need to include them as an appendix in a formal paper; consequently, there is usually a need to re-format them and/or reduce their size to fit within the required margins of a formal paper. The matter is compounded when the scores are printed on paper larger than the standard eight and one-half by eleven-inch page. If at all possible, the score should be reduced to fit the standard eight and one-half by eleven-inch page; the margins must be consistent with the rest of the paper, i.e., a one and one-half inch margin on the left and an inch for all other margins.

In cases where the score is quite large, e.g., a full 26-stave score for which the legibility would be severely impaired by reducing it to fit within the margins of the eight and one-half by eleven-inch page, it may be necessary to consult with a university's graduate office for permission to use an oversized score. This creates problems in binding, particularly when an essay is included with the score, but sometimes this is necessary.

Undoubtedly there are many other format concerns that might be encountered in the preparation of formal music papers, and there usually are several possible solutions for dealing with each. Student writers should consult with their major advisor for guidance in these matters. The underlying principle for dealing with most problems related to format, however, should be to foster clarity of presentation and understanding.

❖ 6 ❖
Documentation: Format Concerns

This chapter is intended to supplement the two style manuals discussed in Chapter 2: *A Manual for Writers of Term Papers, Theses, and Dissertations* (Turabian 1996) and the *Publication Manual of the American Psychological Association* (APA 2001). Besides providing sample formats for citing musical recordings and scores, it also includes examples for three other types of citations that have proven especially troublesome for music students: (a) doctoral dissertations, (b) articles from an encyclopedia, and (c) electronic sources. For the most part, the sample formats are consistent with the sample formats provided in the Turabian and APA style manuals for books, journals, magazines, and various other types of documents. Because the two style manuals use slightly different formats for citing sources, samples formats are provided for each.

Sample Documentation for Recordings (Turabian)

Records, tapes, compact discs, and other forms of recorded sound are entered under the name of the composer for classical music. Collections or anonymous works are listed under title. For jazz and popular music, they are entered under the main performer. When there is doubt, the library's catalog should be consulted and followed. Titles of compositions or titles of the album should be italicized. To cite a single selection from a recording, e.g., one song, the title of the selection should be in quotes, followed by the album title in *italics*.

The names of performers follow the title, similar to the standard form used in discographies: names of soloists followed by names of instrument or voice, name of large ensemble (orchestra, chorus, etc.), name of conductor. The name of the recording company and number of the recording are the major identifying elements. The date, if available on the recording, follows. If the date is found in an outside reference source, it should be in brackets, e.g., [1958]. Lastly, the format of the recording should be indicated: Compact disc, Cassette, LP recording, etc.

Basic Form

Reference List

Last name of composer, First name. Year. *Title in italics.* Soloist, instrument; Large ensemble; Name of conductor. Label name LABEL NUMBER. Format of recording.

Footnote

First name of composer, Last name. *Title in Italics,* Soloist, instrument; Large ensemble; Name of conductor; Label name LABEL NUMBER, Year, format of recording.

Bibliography

Last name of composer, First name. *Title in Italics.* Soloist, instrument; Large ensemble; Name of conductor. Label name LABEL NUMBER, Year. Format of recording.

Title with Genre Name

Reference List

Beethoven, Ludwig van. 1970. *Symphony no. 5 in C minor, op. 67.* Chicago Symphony Orchestra; Seiji Ozawa, conductor. RCA Red Seal LSC 3132. LP recording.

Footnote

Ludwig van Beethoven, *Symphony No. 5 in C minor, Op. 67,* Chicago Symphony Orchestra; Seiji Ozawa, conductor; RCA Red Seal LSC 3132, 1970, LP recording.

Bibliography

Beethoven, Ludwig van. *Symphony No. 5 in C Minor, Op. 67.* Chicago Symphony Orchestra; Seiji Ozawa, conductor. RCA Red Seal LSC 3132, 1970. LP recording.

One Selection from a Collection

Reference List

Copland, Aaron. 1988. "Old American songs," on *Copland Conducts Copland.* William Warfield, baritone; Columbia Symphony Orchestra; Aaron Copland, conductor. CBS Records MK 42430. Compact disc.

Footnote

Aaron Copland, "Old American Songs," on *Copland Conducts Copland,* William Warfield, baritone; Columbia Symphony Orchestra; Aaron Copland, conductor; CBS Records MK 42430, 1988, compact disc.

Bibliography

Copland, Aaron. "Old American Songs," on *Copland Conducts Copland.* William Warfield, baritone; Columbia Symphony Orchestra; Aaron Copland, conductor. CBS Records MK 42430, 1988. Compact disc.

Excerpt from One Piece from a Collection

Reference List

Shostakovich, Dmitri. 1994. "Allegretto," from *Concerto for violoncello and orchestra no. 1 in E flat major, op. 107,* on *Nathaniel Rosen in concert.* Nathaniel Rosen, violoncello; Sofia Philharmonic Orchestra; Emil Tabakov, conductor. John Marks Records JMR 3. Compact disc.

Footnote

Dmitri Shostakovich, "Allegretto," from *Concerto for Violoncello and Orchestra No. 1 in E Flat Major, Op. 107,* on *Nathaniel Rosen in Concert,* Nathaniel Rosen, violoncello; Sofia Philharmonic Orchestra; Emil Tabakov, conductor; John Marks Records JMR 3, 1994, compact disc.

Bibliography

Shostakovich, Dmitri. "Allegretto," from *Concerto for Violoncello and Orchestra No.1 in E Flat Major, Op. 107,* on *Nathaniel Rosen in Concert.* Nathaniel Rosen, violoncello; Sofia Philharmonic Orchestra; Emil Tabakov, conductor. John Marks Records JMR 3, 1994. Compact disc.

Collection Entered under Title

Reference List

Renaissance lute: Music from Italy, England, France, Germany, Spain, and Poland. 1976. Konrad Ragossnig, Renaissance lute. Deutsche Grammophon 413 665-4. Cassette.

Footnote

Renaissance Lute: Music from Italy, England, France, Germany, Spain, and Poland, Konrad Ragossnig, Renaissance lute, Deutsche Grammophon 413 665-4, 1976, cassette.

Bibliography

Renaissance Lute: Music from Italy, England, France, Germany, Spain, and Poland.   Konrad Ragossnig, Renaissance lute.   Deutsche Grammophon 413 665-4, 1976.   Cassette.

Jazz Recording Entered under Performer

Reference List

Blakey, Art. [1959-60]. *Meet you at the jazz corner of the world.* Art Blakey, drums, and the Jazz Messengers. Blue Note BST 84054-84055. 2 LP recordings.

Footnote

Art Blakey, *Meet You at the Jazz Corner of the World,* Art Blakey, drums, and the Jazz Messengers; Blue Note BST 84054-84055, [1959-60], 2 LP recordings.

Bibliography

Blakey, Art. *Meet You at the Jazz Corner of the World.* Art Blakey, drums, and the Jazz Messengers. Blue Note BST 84054-84055, [1959-60]. 2 LP recordings.

Jazz Collection (Entire Work Cited)

Reference List

Smithsonian collection of classic jazz. Rev. ed. 1987. CBS Special Products RD 033. 5 Compact discs.

Footnote

Smithsonian Collection of Classic Jazz, rev. ed., CBS Special Products RD 033, 1987, 5 compact discs.

Bibliography

Smithsonian Collection of Classic Jazz, rev. ed. CBS Special Products RD 033, 1987. 5 Compact discs.

Jazz Excerpt from a Collection

Reference List

Smith, Bessie. 1987. "Lost your head blues," on *Smithsonian collection of classic jazz.* Rev. ed. Bessie Smith, vocals; Joe Smith, cornet; Fletcher Henderson, piano.CBS Special Products RD 033. Disc 1 of 5 compact discs.

Footnote

Bessie Smith, "Lost Your Head Blues," on *Smithsonian Collection of Classic Jazz,* rev. ed., Bessie Smith, vocals; Joe Smith, cornet; Fletcher Henderson, piano; CBS Special Products RD 033, 1987, on disc 1 of 5 compact discs.

Bibliography

Smith, Bessie. "Lost Your Head Blues," on *Smithsonian Collection of Classic Jazz*, rev. ed. Bessie Smith, vocals; Joe Smith, cornet; Fletcher Henderson, piano. CBS Special Products RD 033, 1987. Disc 1 of 5 compact discs.

Video-recording (Spoken)

Reference List

Reed, Alfred. 1986. *Copyright, the law, and you!* Produced by Larry McCormick. 120 min. McCormick's Sharper Images. 2 Videocassettes.

Footnote

Alfred Reed, *Copyright, the Law, and You!* produced by Larry McCormick, 120 min., McCormick's Sharper Images, 1986, 2 videocassettes.

Bibliography

Reed, Alfred. *Copyright, the Law, and You!* Produced by Larry McCormick. 120 min. McCormick's Sharper Images, 1986. 2 Videocassettes.

Citing Notes Accompanying a Recording

When citing notes that accompany a recording, the entry should be under the name of the person writing the notes.

Reference List

Schubert, Giselher. 1996. Program notes for Paul Hindemith's *Das Unaufhörliche*. Ulrike Sonntag, soprano; Robert Worle, tenor; Siegfried Lorenz, baritone; Arthur Korn, bass; Berlin Radio Symphony Orchestra; Lothar Zagrosek, conductor. Wergo WER 6603-2. 2 Compact discs.

Footnote

Giselher Schubert, Program notes for Paul Hindemith's *Das Unaufhörliche*, Ulrike Sonntag, soprano; Robert Worle, tenor; Siegfried Lorenz, baritone; Arthur Korn, bass; Berlin Radio Symphony Orchestra; Lothar Zagrosek, conductor; Wergo WER 6603-2, 1996, 2 compact discs.

Bibliography

Schubert, Giselher. Program notes for Paul Hindemith's *Das Unaufhörliche*. Ulrike Sonntag, soprano; Robert Worle, tenor; Siegfried Lorenz, baritone; Artur Korn, bass; Berlin Radio Symphony Orchestra; Lothar Zagrosek, conductor. Wergo WER 6603-2, 1996. 2 compact discs.

Sample Documentation for Scores (Turabian)

Citations for scores are very similar to those for books. They are entered under the name of the composer. Any other persons responsible for editing, translating, writing the libretto, etc. are placed after the title. A collection that has an editor is entered under the editor's name. If there is no author or editor, the entry is under the title. In general, the title of a score, a large-scale composition, or a collection of smaller pieces should be italicized. For an excerpt from a larger work, e.g., a song or the title of one movement, the title of the excerpt should be in quotations.

Following the composer, title, other editors, etc. is the publication information: place, publisher, and date. If there is more than one place listed, the first place should be entered. If the first place is a U.S. city, it is not necessary to include any other location. If the first place is outside of the U.S., and one of the other places is in the U.S., include both locations. When transcribing the publisher's name, use the shortest recognizable form of the name. Abbreviations such as "Inc.," "Ltd.," "& Sons" should be omitted. Many older scores do not have dates. The abbreviation [n.d.] in brackets is used to indicate no date, or an approximate date may be supplied in brackets, e.g., [19—] or [196-?].

Basic Form

Reference List

Last name of composer, First name. Year. *Title in italics.* Other people responsible for translating, writing the words, etc. Location: Publisher.

Footnote

First name, Last name, *Title in Italics,* other people responsible for translating, writing the words, etc. (Location: Publisher, Year), p. number(s).

Bibliography

Last name, First name. *Title in Italics.* Other people responsible for translating, writing the words, etc. Location: Publisher, Year.

Score with Librettist and Translator

Reference List

Mozart, Wolfgang Amadeus. 1947. *The Marriage of Figaro.* Words by Lorenzo da Ponte, English version by Edward J. Dent, vocal score by Erwin Stein. New York: Boosey & Hawkes.

Footnote

Wolfgang Amadeus Mozart, *The Marriage of Figaro,* words by Lorenzo da Ponte, English version by Edward J. Dent, vocal score by Erwin Stein (New York: Boosey & Hawkes, 1947), 150.

Bibliography

Mozart, Wolfgang Amadeus. *The Marriage of Figaro.* Words by Lorenzo da Ponte, English version by Edward J. Dent, vocal score by Erwin Stein. New York: Boosey & Hawkes, 1947.

Song in a Collection, and Reprint of Original Edition

Reference List

Faure, Gabriel. 1990. Le papillon et la fleur. In *Sixty songs.* Paris, J. Hamelle, 1879. Reprint, New York: Dover.

Footnote

Gabriel Faure, "Le Papillon et la Fleur," in *Sixty Songs* (Paris: J. Hamelle, 1879; reprint, New York: Dover, 1990), 95-99.

Bibliography

Faure, Gabriel. "Le Papillon et la Fleur." In *Sixty Songs.* Paris: J. Hamelle, 1879. Reprint, New York: Dover, 1990.

Collection Entered under Editor

Reference List

Lucktenberg, George, ed. 1988. *The Alienor harpsichord book.* Chapel Hill, N.C.: Hinshaw Music.

Footnote

George Lucktenberg, ed., *The Alienor Harpsichord Book* (Chapel Hill, N.C.: Hinshaw Music, 1988), 55.

Bibliography

Lucktenberg, George, ed. *The Alienor Harpsichord Book.* Chapel Hill, N.C.: Hinshaw Music, 1988.

Sample Documentation for Doctoral Dissertations or Essays (Turabian)

Doctoral Dissertations or Essays [9]

Reference List

Griffin, Malcolm Joseph. 1972. Style and dimension in the choral works of William Schuman. D.M.A. essay, University of Illinois at Champaign-Urbana. Abstract in *Dissertation Abstracts* 33 (1973): 348A.

Moore, James Walter. 1984. A study of tonality in selected works by Leonard Bernstein. Ph.D. diss., The Florida State University. Abstract in *Dissertation Abstracts International* 45 (1985): 2690A.

Footnote

Malcolm Joseph Griffin, "Style and Dimension in the Choral Works of William Schuman" (D.M.A. essay, University of Illinois at Champaign-Urbana, 1972), abstract in *Dissertation Abstracts* 33 (1973): 348A.

James Walter Moore, "A Study of Tonality in Selected Works by Leonard Bernstein" (Ph.D. diss., The Florida State University, 1984), abstract in *Dissertation Abstracts International* 45 (1985): 2690A.

Bibliography

Griffin, Malcolm Joseph. "Style and Dimension in the Choral Works of William Schuman." D.M.A. essay, University of Illinois at Champaign-Urbana, 1972. Abstract in *Dissertation Abstracts* 33 (1973): 348A.

Moore, James Walter. "A Study of Tonality in Selected Works by Leonard Bernstein." Ph.D. diss., The Florida State University, 1984. Abstract in *Dissertation Abstracts International* 45 (1985): 2690A.

Sample Documentation for an Article from an Encyclopedia (Turabian)

Article from an Encyclopedia [10]

Reference List

Jackson, Richard. 1980. Bernstein, Leonard. In *The New Grove Dictionary of Music and Musicians,* ed. Stanley Sadie, vol. 2, 629-631. London: Macmillan.

Footnote

Richard Jackson, "Bernstein, Leonard," in *The New Grove Dictionary of Music and Musicians,* ed. Stanley Sadie (London: Macmillan, 1980), vol. 2, 629-631.

Bibliography

Jackson, Richard. "Bernstein, Leonard." In *The New Grove Dictionary of Music and Musicians,* ed. Stanley Sadie, vol. 2, 629-631. London: Macmillan, 1980.

Sample Documentation for Electronic Documents (Turabian)

Guidelines for citing electronic documents are provided in the Turabian (1996) manual. See pp. 158-159 for sample footnotes and p. 210 for sample bibliography. For other examples see *Electronic Styles: A Handbook for Citing Electronic Information,* by Xia Li and Nancy B. Crane (1996). Additional examples can be found on the following web sites:

http://www.wisc.edu/writing/Handbook/electronic.html

http://www.bridgew.edu/Library/turabian.htm

On-line Article in Scholarly Journal

Reference List

Kelton, Mary Katherine. 1996. Mrs. H. H. A. Beach and her songs for solo voice. *Journal of Singing* 52, no. 3: 3-23, January-February. In *IIMP Full Text* [database on-line]; available from http://iimpft.chadwyck.com/iimp/; Internet (Alexandria, VA: Chadwyck-Healey, accessed 27 June 2003).

Footnote

Mary Katherine Kelton, "Mrs. H. H. A. Beach and Her Songs for Solo Voice, *Journal of Singing* 52, no. 3: 3-23, January-February 1996, in *IIMP Full Text* [database on-line]; available from http://iimpft.chadwyck.com/iimp/; Internet (Alexandria, VA: Chadwyck-Healey, accessed 27 June 2003).

Bibliography

Kelton, Mary Katherine. "Mrs. H. H. A. Beach and Her Songs for Solo Voice." *Journal of Singing* 52, no. 3: 3-23, January-February 1996. In *IIMP Full Text* [database on-line]; available from http://iimpft.chadwyck.com/iimp/; Internet (Alexandria, VA: Chadwyck-Healey, accessed 27 June 2003).

On-line Article in a Magazine

Reference List

Waller, Don. 1999. Jazz goes to college. *Billboard* 111: H14-H15, 1 May. In *Academic Search Elite* [database on-line]; available from http://www.epnet.com/ehost/login.html; Internet (Boston, MA: EBSCO Publishing, accessed 27 June 2003).

Footnote

Don Waller, "Jazz Goes to College," *Billboard* 111: H14-H15, 1 May 1999, in *Academic Search Elite* [database on-line]; available from http://www.epnet.com/ehost/login.html; Internet (Boston, MA: EBSCO Publishing, accessed 27 June 2003).

Bibliography

Waller, Don. "Jazz Goes to College." *Billboard* 111: H14-H15, 1 May 1999. In *Academic Search Elite* [database on-line]; available from http://www.epnet.com/ehost/login.html; Internet (Boston, MA: EBSCO Publishing, accessed 27 June 2003).

On-line Article in a Newspaper

Reference List

Harmon, A. 1996. "Have laptop, will track each blip in the market," *New York Times on the Web*, 6 September [newspaper on-line] available from http://www.nytimes.com/library/tech/98/09/biztech/articles/06tick.html; Internet; accessed 27 June 2003.

Footnote

A. Harmon, "Have Laptop, Will Track Each Blip in the Market," *New York Times on the Web*, 6 September 1996 [newspaper on-line]; available from http://www.nytimes.com/library/tech/98/09/biztech/articles/06tick.html; Internet; accessed 27 June 2003.

Bibliography

Harmon, A. "Have Laptop, Will Track Each Blip in the Market." *New York Times on the Web*, 6 September 1996 [newspaper on-line]; available from http://www.nytimes.com/library/tech/98/09/biztech/articles/06tick.html; Internet; accessed 27 June 2003.

On-line Abstracts

Reference List

Weintraub, L. 1997. "Inner-city post-traumatic stress disorder." *Journal of Psychiatry and Law*, 25, no. 2: 249-286, Summer. Abstract from *PsycLIT* [database on-line]. Accession number: 1998-01611-002.

Footnote

L. Weintraub, "Inner-city Post-Traumatic Stress Disorder," *Journal of Psychiatry and Law*, 25, no. 2: 249-286, Summer 1997, abstract from *PsycLIT* [database on-line], accession number: 1998-01611-002.

Bibliography

Weintraub, L. "Inner-city Post-Traumatic Stress Disorder." *Journal of Psychiatry and Law*, 25, no. 2: 249-286, Summer 1997. Abstract from *PsycLIT* [database on-line]. Accession number: 1998-01611-002.

Professional Web Site

Reference List

Johnson, Michael. 1999. *Vocal jazz resource* [on-line] available from http://www.jazzvocal.com; Internet, accessed 27 June 2003.

Footnote

Michael Johnson, *Vocal Jazz Resource*, 1999 [on-line] available from http://www.jazzvocal.com; Internet, accessed 27 June 2003.

Bibliography

Johnson, Michael. *Vocal Jazz Resource*. 1999. [on-line] available from http://www.jazzvocal.com; Internet, accessed 27 June 2003.

E-mail Communication

Reference List

Boyle, J. David. dboyle@miami.edu. 1999. "Suggestions for graduate handbook." E-mail to Nancy Zavac (nzavac@miami.edu) 8 July.

Footnote

J. David Boyle, dboyle@miami.edu, "Suggestions for Graduate Handbook," e-mail to Nancy Zavac, nzavac@miami.edu, 8 July 1999.

Bibliography

Boyle, J. David. dboyle@miami.edu. "Suggestions for Graduate Handbook." E-mail to Nancy Zavac (nzavac@miami.edu) 8 July 1999.

Sample Documentation for Recordings (APA Style)

Records, tapes, compact discs, and other forms of recorded sound are entered under the name of the composer for classical music. Collections or anonymous works are listed under title. For jazz and popular music, they are entered under the main performer. When there is doubt, the library's catalog should be consulted and followed. Titles for the entire album are italicized. A portion of an album, e.g., one song, is not italicized, underlined, or put in quotes.

The names of the performers follow the title, similar to the standard form used in discographies: names of soloists followed by name of instrument or voice, name of large ensemble, such as orchestra, chorus, etc., name of conductor. It is recommended that the record number be included after the designation of the recording medium (CD, LP or cassette). If the number is included, the medium and number should be in parentheses; if the number is not listed, the medium should be in brackets, e.g., [CD]. The last element includes place of publication and label name taken from the disc itself.

Basic Form (with Genre Name)

Composer's last name, [Initials of given name]. (Year). *Title of major composition or album title* [Recorded by Soloist, instrument; Large ensemble; Conductor]. [Format of recording: CD, record, cassette, etc. LABEL NUMBER]. Location: Label.

Basic Form (One Piece from a Collection)

Composer's last name, [Initials of given name]. (Year). Title of piece or excerpt, from *Title of major composition* [Recorded by Soloist, instrument; Large ensemble; Conductor]. On *Title of album or title of major composition* [Format of recording LABEL NUMBER]. Location: Label.

Title with Genre Name

Beethoven, L. (1970). *Symphony no. 5 in C minor, op. 67* [Recorded by the Chicago Symphony Orchestra; Seiji Ozawa, conductor]. [LP recording LSC 3132]. New York: RCA Red Seal.

One Piece from a Collection

Copland, A. (1988). Old American songs [Recorded by William Warfield, baritone; Columbia Symphony Orchestra; Aaron Copland, conductor]. On *Copland conducts Copland* [CD recording MK 42430]. New York: CBS Records.

Excerpt from a Piece from a Collection

Shostakovich, D. (1994). Allegretto, from *Concerto for violoncello and orchestra no. 1 in E flat major, op. 107* [Recorded by Nathaniel Rosen, violoncello; Sofia Philharmonic Orchestra; Emil Tabakov, conductor]. On *Nathaniel Rosen in concert* [CD recording JMR 3]. Wakefield, RI: John Marks Records.

Collection Entered under Title

Renaissance lute: Music from Italy, England, France, Germany, Spain, and Poland (1976). [Recorded by Konrad Ragossnig]. [Cassette recording 413 665-4]. Germany: Deutsche Grammophon.

Jazz Recording Entered under Performer

Blakey, A. (1959-60). *Meet you at the jazz corner of the world* [Recorded by Art Blakey and the Jazz Messengers]. [LP recordings BST 84054-84055]. New York: Blue Note.

Jazz Collection (Entire Work Cited)

Smithsonian collection of classic jazz (Rev. ed.) (1987). [5 CD recordings RD 033]. New York: CBS Special Products.

Excerpt from a Jazz Collection

Smith, B. (1987). Lost your head blues [Recorded by Bessie Smith, vocals; Joe Smith, cornet; Fletcher Henderson, piano]. On *Smithsonian collection of classic jazz* (Rev. ed.). [Disc 1 of 5 CD recordings RD 033]. New York: CBS Special Products.

Video-recording (Spoken)

Reed, A. (Speaker). (1986). *Copyright, the law, and you!* [Videocassettes]. Arlington Heights, IL: McCormick's Sharper Images.

Citing Notes Accompanying a Recording

When citing notes that accompany a recording, the entry should be under the name of the person writing the notes.

Schubert, G. (1996). Program notes for Paul Hindemith's *Das Unaufhorliche* [Recorded by Ulrike Sonntag, soprano; Robert Worle, tenor; Siegfried Lorenz, baritone; Artur Korn, bass; Berlin Radio Symphony Orchestra; Lothar Zagrosek, conductor] [CD recording WER 6603-2]. Mainz, Germany: Wergo.

Samples for Documentation of Scores
(APA Reference List Style)

Basic Form

Composer's last name, [Initials of given name]. (Year). *Title in italics.* (Name of translator, librettist, etc.). Location: Publisher.

Score with Librettist and Translator

Mozart, W. A. (1947). *The marriage of Figaro.* (L. da Ponte, Librettist, E.J. Dent, Trans., E. Stein, Vocal score). New York: Boosey & Hawkes.

Song in a Collection, Foreign Title, and Reprint of Original Edition

Faure, G. (1990). Le papillon et la fleur [The butterfly and the flower]. In *Sixty songs.* New York: Dover. (Original work published 1879)

Collection Entered under Editor

Lucktenberg, G. (Ed.) (1988). *The Alienor harpsichord book.* Chapel Hill, NC: Hinshaw Music.

Sample Documentation for Doctoral Dissertations or Essays (APA) [11]

Doctoral Dissertations or Essays Abstracted in *Dissertation Abstracts* and Obtained from University Microfilm

Griffin, M. J. (1972). Style and dimension in the choral works of William Schuman. *Dissertation Abstracts, 33* (01), 348A. (UMI No. AAG72-19835)

Moore, J. W. (1984). A study of tonality in selected works by Leonard Bernstein. *Dissertation Abstracts International, 45* (09), 2690A. (UMI No. AAG84-27317)

Doctoral Dissertations or Essays Abstracted in *Dissertation Abstracts* and Obtained from the University

Griffin, M. J. (1972). Style and dimension in the choral works of William Schuman. (Doctoral essay, University of Illinois at Urbana-Champaign, 1972). *Dissertation Abstracts, 33* (01), 348A.

Moore, J. W. (1984). A study of tonality in selected works by Leonard Bernstein. (Doctoral dissertation, The Florida State University, 1984). *Dissertation Abstracts International, 45* (09), 2690A.

Sample Documentation for an Article in an Encyclopedia (APA) [12]

Article in an Encyclopedia

Schiff, D. (2001). Bernstein, Leonard. In *The New Grove dictionary of music and musicians* (2nd ed.). (Vol. 3, pp. 444-449). London: Macmillan.

Sample Documentation for Electronic Documents (APA)

Guidelines for citing electronic documents are provided in the APA style manual (2001); see pp. 268-281 for the APA sample reference list format. For other examples see *Electronic Styles: A Handbook for Citing Electronic Information*, by Xia Li and Nancy B. Crane (1996). Further examples can be found on the following web sites:

http://www.apastyle.org/elecref.html

http://www.wisc.edu/writing/Handbook/DocAPA.html

http://www.bedfordstmartins.com/online/cite6.html

Each entry in a "References" list should include the author, year of publication (in parentheses), title, and publishing data. One should follow the regular APA guidelines for these elements. In addition, electronic citations should contain the form, availability (i.e., location), and date that the electronic source was accessed by the writer.

Basic Form

Author's Last Name, Initial(s). (Year). Title of work or article. Title of Complete Work [if applicable]. Retrieved *date of retrieval* from name of aggregated database/organization or URL.

On-line Article in Scholarly Journal

Kelton, M. K. (1996). Mrs. H. H. A. Beach and her songs for solo voice. *Journal of Singing, 52*, 3-23. Retrieved June 27, 2003, from IIMP Full Text database.

On-line Article in a Magazine

Waller, D. (1999, May 1). Jazz goes to college. *Billboard.* Retrieved June 27, 2003, from Academic Search Elite database.

On-line Article in a Newspaper

Ellison, C. (2002, July 21). Music; when lady and troubadour become one. *New York Times.* Retrieved June 27, 2003, from http://www.nytimes.com

On-line Abstracts

Silverman, M. J. (2003). Contingency songwriting to reduce combativeness and non-cooperation in a client with schizophrenia: A case study. *Arts in Psychotherapy, 30,* 25-33. Abstract retrieved June 27, 2003, from PsychINFO database.

Professional Web Site

Walker, J. R., & Taylor, T. (1998). *Columbia Guide to Online Style.* Retrieved June 27, 2003, from http://www.columbia.edu/cu/cup/cgos/idx_basic.html

Johnson, M. (1999). *Vocal jazz resource.* Retrieved June 27, 2003 from http://www.jazzvocal.com

E-mail Communication

Note: As indicated on p. 214 of the *Publication Manual of the American Psychological Association,* personal communications, whether electronic or other, should not be included in APA-style reference lists because they do not provide recoverable data.

❊ 7 ❊
Enhancing a Text Through the Use
of Simple Music Notation

The clarity of a paper often may be enhanced through judicious use of simple music notation in the text and/or the inclusion of relevant musical examples. In many instances, the inclusion of a brief aspect of music notation in the text may help to make or clarify a point about the music under discussion without having to include a formal musical example. A reference to a specific pitch, key name, chord name, simple rhythm pattern, or tempo indication often facilitates both the flow of the writing and a reader's understanding of the discussion.

Including references to a specific pitch, key name, chord name, simple rhythm pattern, or tempo indication in a text, while seemingly simple, often is challenging to writers working in traditional word-processing programs, partially because some of the necessary fonts are not available. In other instances, it is merely a matter of learning to use some additional aspect of one's word-processing program, particularly the use of *Text Boxes.*

Persons accomplished in using sophisticated music-notation programs such as *Finale 2003a* (MakeMusic! Inc. 2002) may find the incorporation of notation into a text to be a relatively simple task. Many graduate students, however, lack such knowledge and may be dismayed at the prospect of incorporating even simple aspects of notation into a text. This chapter provides information and guidelines for incorporating selected aspects of notation into a text. For convenience, they are discussed as they relate to *pitch-related* and *rhythm-related* aspects of notation. Prior to these discussions, however, a brief note about the use of music notation fonts in a word-processing program seems warranted.

Inserting Music Notation Fonts in Microsoft® Word

To write simple music notation while using Microsoft® Word, one must first install a font that has music notation symbols. Several fonts with music notation symbols appropriate for inclusion in a word-processed text are now available, but because *Finale* appears to have become the "industry standard" for music notation programs, examples discussed here are drawn from it. A current version of *Finale* (*Finale 2003a,* MakeMusic! Inc. 2002), for example, includes three music notation "font character sets": *Maestro, EngraverFont,* and *Jazz,* each of which has several subsets. Because each font character set functions in essentially the same manner, only one, the *Maestro* font, will be used for illustrative purposes.

Before using a music notation font as part of one's word processing program, however, the music notation fonts must be loaded into the font folder of the word processor. In order to know which key to strike for which character (musical symbol), one also must develop a *Font Key Stroke* chart for the music font. A *Font Key Stroke* chart for *Maestro* is included in Appendix D. (If one already is familiar with using *Finale,* this will not be necessary, since the keystrokes for the music symbols are the ones used in typing the symbols while using *Finale.*) If one does not have experience using *Finale,* a little practice will be necessary. With practice, the basic logic of the key strokes will soon become apparent for most of the symbols, e.g., "q" for quarter note, "h" for half note, and "e" for eighth note, with stem directions changing when using upper and lower case letters, i.e., when using or not using "shift" on the computer keyboard.

Once one has gained a certain facility in using the font key strokes for the music characters, it is a relatively simple matter to type the desired symbols. However, inserting them into a document using regular *Times New Roman* or some other text font without creating line spacing problems is another matter.

Using Simple Music Notation in the Text

Pitch-related Aspects

In analyzing or discussing the structural, musical, and peda-gogical aspects of a piece, it often is necessary to refer to specif-ic pitches. A number of systems of *staveless notation* have been used over the years, but the diversity of systems sometimes leads to confusion as to a specific octave designation, even for highly knowledgeable readers. To alleviate this problem, pitch *names* should be specified using octave designations that conform to the piano keyboard. Thus, pitches within the octave above middle C are in the fourth octave of the keyboard and are designated with a subscript 4, e.g., $F\#_4$, G_4, or Bb_4. Pitches in the octave below middle C are in the third octave and thus are designated as D_3 or Eb_3. Campbell and Greated (1987) note that the *staveless notation* system recommended here is consistent with the system adopted by the USA Standards Institute (1960). Young's (1952) summary of the various systems is shown in Appendix F.

Flats and sharps should be designated using the symbols rather than writing out the words; thus, one would write C, Eb, or F#. If necessary for clarity, the symbol for a natural sign should be used, e.g., B♮, E♮, or A♮ (or if it seems more appropriate, B(♮), E(♮), or A(♮)). Some word-processing programs will have fonts for these symbols, although they are not in *Times New Roman*. The symbols for the present manuscript were found in the Microsoft® Word font *MS Reference 1*. (To insert a sharp (#), flat (b), or nat-ural (♮)), one simply changes the active font from *Times New Roman* to *MS Reference 1* (or whatever set of fonts one gets the symbols from), clicks *Insert* on the *Menu Bar*, opens *Symbol*, high-lights the desired symbol, clicks on *insert* and then *close*, and then changes back to *Times New Roman* as the active font.) The use of words in lieu of the symbols is permissible only when the appro-priate fonts are unavailable; they should be designated as follows: E-flat, F-sharp, or B-natural.

Key names should be designated with a capital letter, the appropriate flat or sharp symbol, and the words *major* or *minor.* One should avoid the use of lower case letters for minor keys. Thus, one would write E♭ major or F# minor.

In discussions of traditional harmonic analyses that use chord symbols with the notation, it sometimes is necessary for a writer to refer to a specific chord in the text. Whether to use letter names or Roman numerals usually depends on several factors, including the stylistic era during which the music was composed, the extent of modulation, an advisor's preferences, etc. The system used should be agreed to by the committee chairperson and by any other committee members involved in the supervision of the analysis portion of the paper. The basic concern is that a writer be consistent in the system of symbols used in an analysis.

Beyond the selection of the system for indicating harmonic analysis, a writer has to contend with the difficulty of indicating particular chord structures, which necessarily involves the use of superscripts and subscripts simultaneously such as in a I_4^6 chord. However, one must place the characters within a *Text Box.* The use of text boxes is especially important because a text box allows the notation characters to be sized appropriately for inclusion within a word-processed text. Text boxes are basic to the use of two-level numerals and to the inclusion of simple music notation in a document processed in Microsoft® Word in *Windows.*[13] Text boxes make it possible to insert two-level numerals and certain other aspects of music notation into a word-processed document without disrupting the line spacing. For students who are unfamiliar with the use of Text Boxes, the basic rudiments for using Text Boxes are included in Appendix G.

Chord names in discussions of traditional analyses require the use of either superscripts or the two levels of numerals following the chord name or number, e.g., V^7 or V_4^6 or G^7 or G_4^6. The use of superscript suffices for a single numeral, and the procedure described in Appendix G will suffice for two-level numerals. Sharps and flats will necessarily be needed to indicate altered chords, and symbols for diminished chords (°) should be used if they are available in the font library of one's word processor.

Chord names and *chord spellings* in jazz present a much more complex set of concerns, both in usage and in the notation of them. The extensive use of extended chords, altered chords, slash chords, polychords, etc. creates many challenges for writing about jazz harmonies; further, the writer about jazz harmonies is confronted with diverse traditions in the use of symbols for notating chords. As Miller (1996, 22) notes, "there is a problem with the standardization of modal chord symbols." He goes on to offer a comprehensive system of symbols for indicating jazz chords, but acknowledges that any such system is open to criticism. Students needing to include the names of jazz chords in a text should consult an authoritative source such as Miller's (1996, 1997) two volumes on modal jazz composition and harmony for guidance. Also, one's major advisor will undoubtedly have recommendations about a system to follow. The major concern is consistency, both in the use and notation of chord symbols.

Rhythm-related Aspects

The most common rhythm-related aspects of notation that one may have occasion to use are note and rest values and tempo indications. The particular problem here is twofold: (a) to find a font that includes these symbols and (b) to be able to insert them in the text without creating problems with line spacing. Usually one must insert fonts from a music notation program such as those available in *Finale 2003a* and import them into a Microsoft® Word font folder. The examples below use music fonts from *Maestro* font.

Simply changing to a music font when there is a need to indicate some note or rhythm values in a text, however, does not work, because the use of a music font causes changes in the line spacing. To avoid this problem, one must use *Text Boxes,* which can be sized to fit within the line spacing of the text. For example, if one would like to notate a rhythm pattern such as

$\frac{3}{4}$ ♩ ♩|♩♩|♩♩♩|♩ ‖ it can be accomplished with relative ease by following the steps outlines in Appendix G. Of course, it does require some practice.

Obviously, there are limitations with respect to the music symbols that can be notated within a word processing text. For example, if one desires beamed eighth or sixteenth notes instead of stand-alone notes, one must use quarter notes and, using black ink, simply draw the beams. Also, certain other symbols may not be available.

There often is a need to indicate metronome markings for given pieces or movements of a work. The standard procedure for such indications is M.M. ♩ = 80. (The M.M. is the abbreviation for *Maelzel's Metronome*, not for metronome mark.) If one desires to use the Italian terms, they should be italicized, e.g., *vivace, allegro,* or *largo.*

Other Aspects of Notation

Some aspects of notation that a writer might desire to use do not relate directly to either pitch or rhythm notation, e.g., dynamic markings such as *pp, mf, ff.* These indications should be italicized and bold, just as in standard notation. For such markings one can simply use bold and italics for these terms in *Times New Roman.* As with other aspects of manuscript preparation, the important thing is to be consistent.

A writer may choose to use a variety of other music symbols when writing about music, e.g., clefs 𝄞 𝄢 𝄡 or fermatas 𝄐. Whatever symbols a writer uses, the ultimate concern should be to enhance the clarity of the discussion and the appearance of the manuscript.

Should a writer desire to include actual notation, with clef signs, meter signatures, notes, etc. on an actual staff, then it will be necessary to gain assistance from someone proficient in the use of a music-notation program such as *Finale.* Or, if notation is an important part of a paper and the inclusion of cut-and-paste examples from given scores is insufficient for the type of analysis and discussion one desires to make, then it may be advantageous to learn to use one of the music-notation programs.

❋ 8 ❋
Incorporating Musical Examples, Tables, and Figures

Many times a writer needs to provide detail beyond what can be related in a text, and musical examples, tables, and figures are useful in providing such detail. This chapter provides brief guidelines for including them in a formal paper.

Musical examples are necessary for many papers by music students because they allow the writer to show the actual notation for a passage under discussion. Judicious inclusion of relevant musical examples often enhances discussions of musical analyses, descriptions of performance practices, and presentations of particular pedagogical approaches to a given musical passage. Musical examples usually are considered *formal* in that they include an example number and a caption that specifies the composer, the title of the piece, the movement or section, the inclusive measure numbers, and usually a brief description of the musical attribute under discussion.

Tables are used to provide additional detail for quantitative information beyond that presented in the text. Most tables consist primarily of quantitative data, although occasionally certain types of descriptive data may be summarized conveniently in a *word table* (APA 2001, 161-166). *Figures* provide a means for helping a reader quickly grasp information that is somewhat cumbersome to convey in text; figures may include graphs, charts, illustrations, maps, photographs, or any other visual that may readily clarify or enhance understanding of a topic.

Formal musical examples, tables, and figures should have a number and caption. They may be numbered either by chapter or consecutively throughout the paper. If numbered by chapter, they should include designations for both chapter and number, thus the second musical example in chapter three of a paper would be referred to as Example 3.2. Captions for musical examples and tables are placed above the examples and tables, whereas captions for figures are placed below the figure. If a writer includes musical examples in a paper, a List of Musical Examples must be included in the frontispieces of the paper following the Table of Contents. The complete information for each musical example must be included in the List of Musical Examples. Similarly, if one includes tables and figures in a paper, there must be a separate List of Tables and List of Figures.

There must be an extra space *above* and *below* each musical example, table, and figure, i.e., for musical examples and tables, a triple space above the caption and below the example or table, and for figures, a triple space above the figure and below the caption. The additional spacing is especially important for musical examples and tables in order to set off the caption from the preceding text.

Each musical example, table, and figure must be mentioned in the text *by example, table, or figure number* prior to its inclusion in the paper. Placement of a musical example, table, or figure should be immediately *following* the paragraph in which it is mentioned. If there is insufficient space on the page for the example, table, or figure, it should be placed at the top of the following page. Under no circumstances should it be inserted in the middle of a paragraph. Also, each must be within the confines of the margins established for the text. Musical examples, tables, and figures must not extend into the margins.

The Turabian (1996, chapters 6 and 7) and APA (2001, 147-201) style manuals each provide extensive discussion and examples of tables and figures, including many guidelines for setting up various types of tables and figures. The present discussion, therefore, includes only two examples of each, one in Turabian style and one in APA style. For the most part, differences between Turabian and APA formats for musical examples, tables, and figures are slight. The primary differences relate to the captions, notably centered for Turabian style versus left-justified and italicized caption for APA style. Guidelines for incorporating musical examples into a text are not examined in either manual.

Inserting Musical Examples, Tables, and Figures into Microsoft® Word

Because musical examples, tables, and figures often are set up in files separate from one's word-processed text, it may be helpful to consider the basic procedures for inserting them into the finalized document. Processes for incorporating musical examples, tables, and figures into a word-processed text may vary from the simple cut-and-paste approach to sophisticated applications for linking and embedding documents from one program into another. For example, it often is useful to create statistical tables in Microsoft® Excel and then insert them in the appropriate place in a word-processed text via Microsoft's procedures for linking or embedding objects into a word-processed document. Because the primary concern for music students is the inclusion of musical examples, the procedures outlined here focus on them rather than tables and figures. However, the procedures are applicable to tables and figures to be inserted from other files.

Following are the basic procedures for moving a musical excerpt (or an entire page) from a composition prepared in *Finale 2003a* to a document in Microsoft® Word. It assumes the user has basic knowledge of *Finale 2003a* (or whatever version of *Finale* one is using) and is facile at using pull-down screens in *Microsoft Word*. In *Finale,*

1. Open the musical document from which you wish to export the musical example. Be sure it is in *Page View, Home Position,* and at *100% of Scale.*

2. Open the *Graphics Menu.* (This may require selection of the *Advanced Tools Palette* under the *Windows Menu* and then double clicking on the *Graphics Icon* from the *Advanced Tools Palette.)*

3. Select the portion of the musical document to be exported by double-clicking and dragging the second click around the measure(s) to be exported and releasing the second click once the excerpt is enclosed in the dotted-line box.

4. From the *Graphics Menu*, select *Export Selection*, create a *TIFF* file for it, name it, and save it in a folder in *Finale* where you save your musical documents. In setting up the TIFF file, simply follow the guidelines in the dialog box that appears after selection of *Export Selection*. (If one desires to export a page, select *Export Pages* instead of *Export Selection*; the dialog box will request the page(s) to be selected.)

In Microsoft® Word,

1. Open the document into which the musical excerpt is to be placed, and move the curser to the place in the document where the excerpt is to be placed. (Excerpts can be placed at the left margin, centered, or at the right margin by using the alignment icons.)

2. From the *Insert Menu*, select *Insert Picture* from a *File*. A dialog box will open and request the folder (In *Finale*) from which the excerpt is to be taken. Select the file (as the TIFF file was named in No. 4 above) to be inserted and click on *Insert* in the dialog box. The excerpt should appear at the place of the curser in your Microsoft® Word document.

Format for Musical Examples

Musical examples are especially important for recital papers and other papers in which a writer needs to show a reader a particular musical passage. Captions for musical examples are placed above the example, and there should be no lines above and below musical examples. If a musical example is not taken from public domain and if its source is not clear from the caption, the source should be documented, either in a footnote or as a reference, depending on which system of documentation is being used. A caption for a musical example should clearly identify the composer, work and opus number, movement, particular voice or instrument part, and the inclusive measure numbers of the example. Each example should include relevant clef signs, key signatures, and meter signatures.

If it is necessary to refer a reader to a large section of a work, i.e., more than one page of musical notation, it usually is best to include the section in an appendix. Ordinarily, only musical examples of one page or less should be included in the body of a paper. Appendix H includes two musical examples, paraphrased from student papers (Hall 1998, 64-65; Luce 1995, 89-90). There are Turabian and APA versions of each example. As should be apparent, the differences in the two versions are slight; besides the differences in the captions, the Turabian version centers the example between margins and the APA version places the example flush with the left-hand margin.

Format for Tables

Essentially, a table provides explication of quantitative data. A table follows, and presents in greater detail, a discussion of a particular set of quantitative data in the text. One should avoid trying to discuss all details of a table in the text, since this would make the table superfluous. As for musical examples, the differences in format suggested by the Turabian and APA style manuals are slight. Generally, the Turabian manual recommends centering a table caption and a table on a page, while the APA manual suggests that table captions be flush with the left-hand margin of the table. Each offers several options for use of lines in a table, but, generally and regardless of style manual, it is best to include a horizontal line to mark the beginning and the end of a table. Also, heading information within the table usually is set off with another horizontal line. Unless data are especially complex, vertical lines are not necessary.

Appendix I includes two examples of tables and the paragraphs in which each is mentioned. The examples are paraphrased from student papers (Anspaugh 1999, 38-39; Busse 1997, 77). Turabian and APA examples are provided for each.

Format for Figures

Figures are intended to allow writers to use pictographic information to show relationships and/or synthesize information that may be awkward to convey to a reader in text alone. Figures differ from tables in two basic ways: (a) The content of figures is primarily pictographic rather than quantitative, although quantitative data are sometimes included as part of a figure, and (b) the captions for figures are placed below rather than above the figure.

Some figures (charts and graphs) may even be used to summarize quantitative data in graphic rather than tabular format. Whatever the nature of the figure, it must follow the text's discussion of the information in the figure, and there must be a specific text reference to the figure. Appendix J includes two examples of figures used in student papers and the related text discussion of each (Ngim 1997, 137; Nikolic 1999, 7-8). Turabian and APA models are included for each.

References

American Psychological Association. 2001. *Publication manual of the American Psychological Association.* 5th ed. Washington, DC: APA.

Anspaugh, Erin E. 1999. "Master's recital paper." M.M. paper, University of Miami.

Busse, Walter G. 1997. "Toward objective measurement and evaluation of jazz piano performance via MIDI-based groove quantize templates." Ph.D. diss., University of Miami.

Campbell, Murray, and Clive Greated. 1987. *The musician's guide to acoustics.* New York: Schirmer Books.

The Chicago manual of style. 14th ed. 1993. Chicago: University of Chicago Press.

Hall, Nelson. 1998. "The use of text in three twentieth-century settings of *Psalm 150:* Implications for the conductor. D.M.A. essay, University of Miami.

Helm, E. Eugene, and Albert T. Luper. 1982. *Words and music.* Rev. ed. Totowa, NJ: European American Music Corp.

Li, Xia, and Nancy B. Crane. 1996. *Electronic style: Handbook for citing electronic information.* Medford, NJ: Information Today.

Luce, Lynn Sams. 1995. "William Walton's *Belshazzar's Feast*: A conductor's analysis for performance." D.M.A. essay, University of Miami.

MakeMusic! Inc. 2002. *Finale 2003a.* Eden Prairie, MN: MakeMusic! Inc.

Miller, Ron. 1996, 1997. *Modal jazz: Composition and harmony* (2 vols.). Rottenburg N., Germany: Advance Music.

Montgomery, Michael, and John Stratton. 1981. *The writer's hotline handbook.* New York: The New American Library.

Morris, William, and Mary Morris. 1975. *Harper dictionary of contemporary usage.* New York: Harper and Row.

Ngim, Alan G. 1997. "Olivier Messiaen as a pianist: A study of tempo and rhythm based on his recordings of *Vision de l'amen.*" D.M.A. essay, University of Miami.

Nilolic, Zlatan. 1999. "Applications in commercial music writing and production." M.M. project paper, University of Miami.

Randel, Don Michael. 1986. *The new Harvard dictionary of music.* Cambridge, MA: Belknap Press of Harvard University Press.

Sadie, Stanley, ed. 2001. *The new Grove dictionary of music and musicians.* 2nd ed. London: Macmillan.

Strunk, William, Jr., and E. B. White. 1959. *The elements of style.* New York: Macmillan.

Turabian, Kate L. 1996. *A manual for writers of term papers, theses, and dissertations.* 6th ed. Revised by John Grossman and Alice Bennett. Chicago: University of Chicago Press.

USA Standards Institute. 1960. American standard acoustical terminology, S1.1— New York: USA Standards Institute.

Walters, Darrel. 1999. *The readable thesis: A guide to clear and effective writing.* Gilsum, NH: Avocus Publishing.

Webster's third new international dictionary. 1971. Springfield, MA: G.& C. Merriam.

Young, Robert W. 1952. *A table relating frequency to cents.* Elkhart, IN: C.G. Conn.

Notes

[1]The *Author-Date* system of documentation as described in Chapter 10 of the Turabian manual was used in the preparation of this manual. Chapter 2 of this manual provides an overview of the *Author-Date* and *Footnote-Bibliography* systems of documentation.

[2] The 1996 edition of the Turabian manual conforms to *The Chicago Manual of Style,* 14th ed. (Chicago: The University of Chicago Press, 1993).

[3] Since recital papers differ considerably from other types of graduate research papers, a separate chapter is devoted to the preparation and organization of them; see Chapter 4.

[4]In the authors' institution, the faculty of the classical performance programs (instrumental, keyboard, and vocal) established a policy that master's recital papers must be written and defended in the semester preceding the semester in which the recital is given. This both facilitates students' learning and understanding the recital repertoire while leaving the final preparations of the recital unencumbered by pressures to complete the paper. It also appears to have greatly increased the completion rate for master's degree programs in performance. However, the jazz faculty views the purpose of the master's recital paper differently and does not require the paper to be written prior to the recital. They view it as a retrospective description and analysis of the performance, including descriptions of original compositions and

arrangements performed. Both approaches have recognized merits.

⁵With a committee's approval, a summary chapter sometimes is added after the performance and includes a "self-evaluation" of the recital itself and may include recommendations for changes that might be incorporated into subsequent recitals.

⁶The authors are indebted to Professor Paul Wilson, Ph.D., of the University of Miami School of Music for much of the information in this section.

⁷Users of Microsoft® Word who are accomplished at using *Master Documents* may accomplish this same process by creating a Master Document and Subdocuments. This is a relatively easy process for knowledgeable users of a word processing program; however, persons just learning to use a word processing program might find it easier to simply put each chapter in a separate file and repaginate when all are completed.

⁸Most word processing programs also have procedures for creating a system of headings more-or-less automatically; e.g., Microsoft® Word includes a feature, *Styles*, which may be used for this purpose. Again, for persons relatively new to a word processing program, it may be simpler to just type in the headings.

⁹For dissertations up to volume 35 (1975) use the title *Dissertation Abstracts*. For dissertations in volume 36 (1976) and higher use the title *Dissertation Abstracts International*; for Ph.D., Ed.D., and D.Ed. degree papers use the term "diss." in citation; for D.M.A. papers use the term "essay" in citation; for additional examples see Turabian, 6ᵗʰ ed., pp. 158 and 209.

¹⁰Follow example 11.26 "Component Part by One Author in a Work by Another," Turabian, 6ᵗʰ ed., pp. 196-197.

[11]For dissertations up to volume 35 (1975) use the title *Dissertation Abstracts;* for dissertations in volume 36 (1976) and higher use the title *Dissertation Abstracts International;* for Ph.D., Ed.D., and D.Ed. degree papers use the term "doctoral dissertation" in citation; for D.M.A. papers, use term "doctoral essay" in citation; for further examples see *APA Publication Manual,* 5th ed., pp. 260-262.

[12]Refer to example 38, *APA Publication Manual,* 5th ed., p. 254.

[13]Text boxes are essential for incorporating music fonts into a text, because simply switching to a music font such as *Maestro* without placing the notation in a text box disrupts the line spacing.

APPENDIX A
Sample Introduction for a Recital Paper

Sample Introduction for a Recital Paper

The purpose of this paper is to describe and analyze the repertory selected for a solo piano recital performed by the author in partial fulfillment of the requirements of the Master of Music degree. This introduction serves to describe some of the issues considered in selecting the repertory for performance and provides an overview of the remainder of the recital paper.

The selection of repertory for performance is an arduous task for any musician and is made especially difficult for the student musician due to the many considerations that influence the choices of music. As with any performing musician, the author selected repertory that tends to provide opportunities for her to demonstrate those skills, techniques, and other performance attributes that generally favor the author's individual performance abilities. Historical representativeness was also an important consideration for the selection of music, particularly given the breadth of repertory available for keyboard. Moreover, this recital, as a student recital, functions as a representation of the culmination of musical learning experiences for the author as a performer and as such the repertory selected often represents some of the skills and knowledge gained during formal study at the graduate level. The role of the author's principal applied teacher in the selection of repertory also was an important factor as the selections reflect the basic didactic principles to which he ascribes. These principles include extensive focus on clarity of contrapuntal lines, virtuosic technique, and production of resonant, yet delicate tone. Lastly, the emotional and physical pacing of the recital influenced not only the selection of the music, but the order of presentation in the recital. These considerations have relevance for both the performer and the audience and will be discussed in greater detail in subsequent chapters.

The repertory for this recital included four Scarlatti sonatas (K. 26, K. 96, K. 208, and K. 455), Johann Sebastian Bach's *Partita No. 5*, the *Sonata in B-flat minor*, *Opus 35* by Frédéric Chopin, and the Schuman *Fantasy in C major*. In this paper the author provides a general historical orientation to the repertory selected, and each work is discussed in greater detail in succeeding chapters.

For each selection in the recital, the author presents and discusses the salient historical aspects related to the work, provides an analysis of the musical content, and describes selected aspects of performance practice that the author deems relevant and important. The four Scarlatti sonatas are discussed within a single chapter, partly because of their brevity, but primarily to examine the relationships and differences among these pieces, which reflect selected aspects of Scarlatti's evolution as a keyboard composer and function to define the early development of the keyboard sonata genre.

Each of the remaining works has a separate chapter devoted to it. (etc., etc.)

APPENDIX B
Sample System of Headings

Chapter 1

CHAPTER TITLE IN ALL CAPS

The first line of each chapter should begin on the third line below the chapter title; another way to think of this is as triple spaced. The first level of subheading in a chapter or paper should be centered and may be either in **bold** or in ***bold italics*** with initial capital letters for major words. With the exception of a heading immediately below a chapter title, the spacing above and below each heading should be double spaced, which is the same spacing as used between lines of text. The use of the boldface font is sufficient to call a reader's attention to the heading. In the event a heading is of such length that it requires two lines, the heading should be single spaced.

First-level Subheading: Levels

Headings should help the organization of a paper, making it easier for both the writer and the reader. It is important, however, that headings be relevant and necessary. Overuse of subheadings without clearly defined subtopics should be avoided. This appendix, which is included for illustrative purposes, is an example of overuse of subheadings.

Second-level Subheading: Font

The second level subheading in a chapter is a free standing side heading in either **bold** or ***bold italics***. One should be consistent between levels of subheadings, making them either all **bold** or all ***bold italics***.

Second-level Subheading: Number

Any time a subheading is used in a section of a paper, there must be at least two subheadings at that level. One cannot subdivide a section into fewer than two sections.

Third-level subheading, use of capitals. If one needs a third-level subheading, the indented paragraph heading is used. Just as for the first and second levels, it may be either **bold** or ***bold italics***; it should also be consistent with the font of the first- and second-level headings. However, as shown above, the third-level subheading only requires a capital letter for the first word. Subsequent words are not capitalized.

Third-level subheading, topic. Regardless of the level of a subheading, a second subheading must deal with a different aspect of the topic for that level. Should there not be a clearly definable second aspect of the topic, no subheadings should be used for the section.

APPENDIX C
Sample Frontispieces

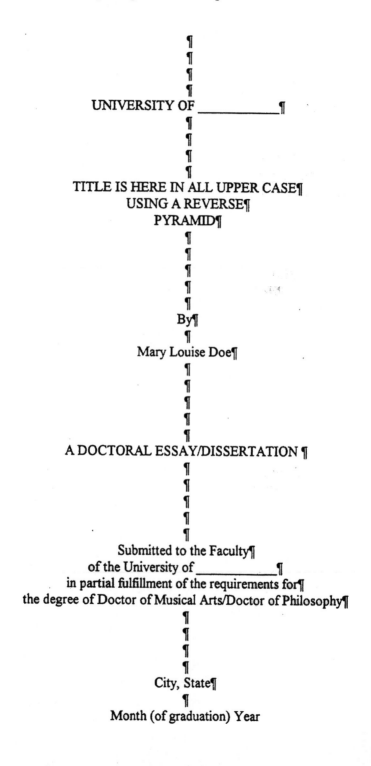

¶
¶
¶
¶
¶

UNIVERSITY OF _____ ¶

¶
¶
¶
¶

TITLE IS HERE IN ALL UPPER CASE¶
USING A REVERSE¶
PYRAMID¶

¶
¶
¶
¶
¶

By¶

¶

Mary Louise Doe¶

¶
¶
¶
¶
¶

A DOCTORAL ESSAY/DISSERTATION ¶

¶
¶
¶
¶
¶

Submitted to the Faculty¶
of the University of _____ ¶
in partial fulfillment of the requirements for¶
the degree of Doctor of Musical Arts/Doctor of Philosophy¶

¶
¶
¶
¶

City, State¶

¶

Month (of graduation) Year

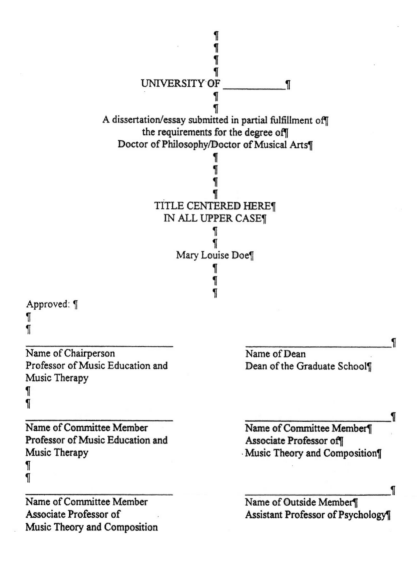

¶
¶
¶
¶
UNIVERSITY OF _____ ¶
¶
¶
A dissertation/essay submitted in partial fulfillment of¶
the requirements for the degree of¶
Doctor of Philosophy/Doctor of Musical Arts¶
¶
¶
¶
¶
TITLE CENTERED HERE¶
IN ALL UPPER CASE¶
¶
¶
Mary Louise Doe¶
¶
¶
¶

Approved: ¶
¶
¶

————————————————   ————————————————¶
Name of Chairperson   Name of Dean
Professor of Music Education and   Dean of the Graduate School¶
Music Therapy
¶
¶

————————————————   ————————————————¶
Name of Committee Member   Name of Committee Member¶
Professor of Music Education and   Associate Professor of¶
Music Therapy   Music Theory and Composition¶
¶
¶

————————————————   ————————————————¶
Name of Committee Member   Name of Outside Member¶
Associate Professor of   Assistant Professor of Psychology¶
Music Theory and Composition

¶
¶
¶
¶
¶
¶
¶
¶
UNIVERSITY OF _____¶
¶
¶
¶
¶
¶
¶
A RECITAL PAPER¶
¶
¶
¶
¶
¶
¶
By¶
¶
Mary Louise Doe¶
¶
¶
¶
¶
¶
¶
Submitted to the Faculty¶
of the University of _____¶
in partial fulfillment of the requirements for¶
the degree of Master of Music¶
¶
¶
¶
¶
City, State¶
¶
Month (of graduation) Year

APPENDIX D
Setting up a Table of Contents in Microsoft® Word

SETTING UP A TABLE OF CONTENTS IN MICROSOFT® WORD

Setting up a Table of Contents in Microsoft® Word offers some real challenges, and the steps listed below are intended to help the cause by offering a "by-the-numbers" approach.

Step

1. Set the standard margins for a paper that is to be bound: 1.5" on the left and 1.0" everywhere else.

2. Set the TABS for the page as follows:

    0.25
    0.50
    0.75
    1.00
    5.60 with leader
    5.80

3. Type **TABLE OF CONTENTS** centered and on the fourth single-spaced line below the top margin.

4. Type the word "Page" on the third line below that and align it to the right.

5. Type LIST OF EXAMPLES, hit the space bar twice, and then hit TAB. The leader should appear as on the following page. Then hit TAB again and type in the page number of the LIST OF EXAMPLES. (If the Table of Contents is a single page, the page number of the List of Examples will be *iv.*)

6. Type the word Chapter on the second line below the LIST OF EXAMPLES.

7. On the second line below the word Chapter, hit TAB and then type 1, the number of the first chapter. Hit TAB again and then type the name of the first chapter. Hit the space bar twice and then hit TAB to get the leader line. Hit TAB again and use space bar to align the page number flush with the right-hand margin.

8. Assuming all goes well, finish typing the page.

TABLE OF CONTENTS

Page

APPENDIX E
Key Strokes: Maestro Font

Key Strokes: Maestro Font

a =	q =	G =	W =	! =	} =
b =	r =	H =	X =	@ =	| =
c =	s =	I =	Y =	# =	; =
d =	t =	J =	Z =	$ =	' =
e =	u =	K =	1 =	% =	: =
f =	v =	L =	2 =	^ =	" =
g =	w =	M =	3 =	& =	, =
h =	x =	N =	4 =	* =	. =
i =	y =	O =	5 =	(=	/ =
j =	z =	P =	6 =	) =	< =
k =	A =	Q =	7 =	_ =	> =
l =	B =	R =	8 =	+ =	? =
m =	C =	S =	9 =	[=	` =
n =	D =	T =	0 =	] =	~ =
o =	E =	U =	- =	\ =	
p =	F =	V =	= =	{ =	

(Key Strokes for Commonly Used Symbols)

Note Values

W = ▯   h = ♩   q = ♩   e = ♪   x = ♪

w = ○   H = ⌐   Q = ⌐   E = ⌐   X = ⌐

. = .   (to add dot for dotted notes; e.g., ♩. ♪ ♩. ♪)

Accidentals

= ♯   b = ♭   n = ♮   a = ⌀   A = ♭   N = ⌀

Clefs, Staff, Bar Line, and Double Bar

& = 𝄞   ? = 𝄢   B = 𝄡   = = ☰   \ = | / = ‖

Meter Signatures

c = 𝄴   C = 𝄵   (for numerals simply use the numerals with .25 line space)

$\begin{smallmatrix}3\\4\end{smallmatrix}$ $\begin{smallmatrix}6\\8\end{smallmatrix}$ $\begin{smallmatrix}4\\4\end{smallmatrix}$

Dynamic Markings

pp = *pp*   p = *p*   P = *mp*   F = *mf*   f = *f*   ff = *ff*

Z = *fz*   S = *sf*

APPENDIX F
Young's Summary of Staveless Notation Systems

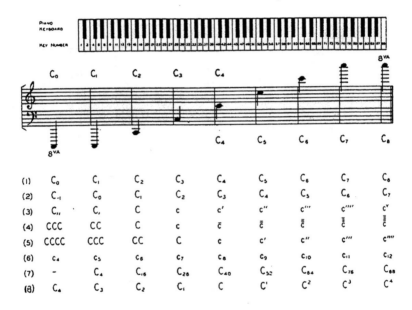

Fig. I. A comparison of staveless notations.

APPENDIX G
Using Text Boxes to Insert Aspects of
Music Notation in a Text

Using Text Boxes to Insert Aspects of
Music Notation in a Text

An assumption of this outline is that a user has at least rudimentary knowledge about using the *Menu Bar* and a *mouse*. **Step 1** involves clicking *Insert* on the *Menu Bar* and opening *Text Box* on the pull-down menu beneath it. (This results in a "cross-hair" [+] which can be converted into a working "highlighted" text box by clicking it with the mouse. The box can be *sized* by clicking one of the small circles on the frame of the box and moving in or out with the mouse; similarly, the box can be *moved* by clicking on the edge of the box and dragging it with the mouse.) With the box open and highlighted, **step 2** involves clicking *Format* on the *Menu Bar* and opening *Text Box* beneath it, which opens the dialog box *Format Text Box*. **Step 3** requires the selection of three *tabs* under *Format Text Box*, (a) clicking the tab *Colors and Lines*, under which one clicks on *colors* and selects "no lines," (b) then clicking the tab *Text Box* and changing the internal left and right margins of the box to 0.0 inches, and (c) then clicking the tab *Position* or *Layout* and making sure there is a check in the box by "move object with text." After this, one should click on "okay" to set these parameters for this box. With the box still highlighted and the cursor in the box, step 4 involves the opening of *Fonts* under *Format* on the menu bar and changing the font size from 12 to 10 for meter signatures and from 12 to 8 for chord inversions. (One may also open *Paragraph* under *Format* and reduce the line spacing from "single" to "multiple" at .8 in order to reduce the space between the upper and lower numbers.) At this point, and given a little trial-and-error, one should be able to create two numerals, one over the other, and place them in the appropriate place in the text, e.g., $\frac{3}{4}$ meter or $\frac{6}{4}$ chord. (After typing the upper numeral, one should hit return and then type the lower numeral immediately below the upper. The size of the text box should be reduced to just fit what is typed in it, and then the box with the numerals in it should be dragged to the appropriate place in the text. To remove the box, simply click outside of the box.) If one encounters difficulties in using the text box, e.g., moving it or changing its size, a review of the basics for using a text box might be in order, including how to anchor a text box to a paragraph. It should be noted, however, that subsequent changes *within* the paragraph and *preceding* the meter signature or the chord symbol will *not* move the text box symbols with the text; one must highlight the text box and drag the numerals to the new location. However, changes in other paragraphs preceding the paragraph with the text box numerals will not disrupt the placement of the symbols.

The steps for inserting a brief rhythm pattern such as $\frac{3}{4}$ ♩♩♩│♩.‖ are quite similar to the steps for creating meter signatures. After entering the meter signature using the steps outlined above, **step 1** involves opening another *Text Box* for the notes by clicking *Insert* on the *Menu Bar* and opening *Text Box* on the pull-down menu beneath it. Once the box is open and highlighted, **step 2** involves clicking *Format* on the *Menu Bar* and opening *Text Box* beneath it, which opens dialog box *Format Text Box*. **Step 3** requires the selection of three tabs under *Format Text Box*, (a) clicking the tab *Colors and Lines*, under which one clicks on *colors* and selects "no lines," (b) then clicking the tab *Text Box* and changing the internal left and right margins of the box to 0.0 inches, and (c) then clicking the tab *Position* or *Layout* and making sure there is a check in the box by "move object with text." After this, one should click on "okay" to set parameters for this box. With the box still highlighted and the cursor still in the box, **step 4** involves changing the font from *Times New Roman* (or whichever font one is using for the text) to *Maestro*. The font size should be changed from 12 to 14. At this point and using the key stroke chart, **step 5** involves simply typing the notes and bar lines as desired. Obviously, the space bar must be used to create the appropriate spacing. Once this is accomplished, **step 6** simply involves reducing the size of the box, dragging it to the appropriate space in the text, moving the cursor outside the text box, and clicking it to remove the visible box from around the notation. While the outlined steps may seem challenging at first, one can with a little bit of practice become quite adept at inserting simple notation into a text.

APPENDIX H
Sample Musical Examples

[Sample No. 1: Turabian-style Musical Example]

The first section, mm. 1-13, written for soprano solo, introduces theme A. The theme consists of a one-measure phrase based on a descending and an ascending melodic line on the "Halleluiah" text (Example 3.1). The melodic line is accompanied by the woodwinds (divisi flute, oboe, clarinet) and horn in a sustained osinato four-chord motive. This pattern and its developmental designs are the unifying ideas for the movement. This opening section, with an F tonal center, also serves as an introduction to the entire composition; its music also returns in *ritornello* fashion in section 3 (mm. 33-42), section 6 (mm. 68-86), and the final (seventh) section (mm. 87-99).

Example 3.1 Heinz Werner Zimmerman, Psalm 150, mvt. 1, mm. 1-3, First section, theme A.

[Sample No. 1: APA-style Musical Example]

The first section, mm. 1-13, written for soprano solo, introduces theme A. The theme consists of a one-measure phrase based on a descending and an ascending melodic line on the "Halleluiah" text (Example 3.1). The melodic line is accompanied by the woodwinds (divisi flute, oboe, clarinet) and horn in a sustained osinato four-chord motive. This pattern and its developmental designs are the unifying ideas for the movement. This opening section, with an F tonal center, also serves as an introduction to the entire composition; its music also returns in *ritornello* fashion in section 3 (mm. 33-42), section 6 (mm. 68-86), and the final (seventh) section (mm. 87-99).

Example 3.1 Heinz Werner Zimmerman, Psalm 150, mvt. 1, mm. 1-3, First section, theme A.

[Sample No. 2: Turabian-style Musical Example]

Example 13 shows five variations on both the original "praise" theme and its derivative. The first variation is in measure 416, with alto and soprano outlining a fragment from the opening "praise" theme. The second and third variations are in the tenor and bass (measure 417), which continue the theme from the first variation, with the tenor omitting the trill. Variation four is an extension of variation one, outlining a triad, this time in three voices (soprano and alto I and II). The fifth variation is also an extension of variation one, ending prematurely in an upward gesture that leaves the listener wanting more.

Example 13. William Walton, *Belshazzar's Feast*, mm. 416-419. Fragmentation of original "Praise" theme (SATB Chorus).

[Sample No. 2: APA-style Musical Example]

Example 13 shows five variations on both the original "praise" theme and its derivative. The first variation is in measure 416, with alto and soprano outlining a fragment from the opening "praise" theme. The second and third variations are in the tenor and bass (measure 417), which continue the theme from the first variation, with the tenor omitting the trill. Variation four is an extension of variation one, outlining a triad, this time in three voices (soprano and alto I and II). The fifth variation is also an extension of variation one, ending prematurely in an upward gesture that leaves the listener wanting more.

Example 13. William Walton, *Belshazzar's Feast*, mm. 416-419. Fragmentation of original "Praise" theme (SATB Chorus).

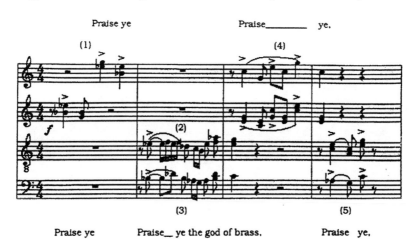

APPENDIX I
Sample Tables

[Sample No. 1: Turabian-style Table]

The third movement, "*Adagio Mesto,*" initially appears to have little formal structure, but upon closer examination, there is a high degree of formal structure. The overall form of the movement is ABA, but it could also be viewed as having a sonata-allegro form. There are two themes that have expositions, a development section, and a recapitulation of the first theme, which returns to the home key of El minor and ends with a coda. Table 3.14 outlines the form of the movement.

Table 3.14. Brahms, *Trio for violin, horn, and piano,*
Op. 40, Mvt. 3, Form

Sections	Subsections	Measures	Keys
Theme I (A)	a motive	1 - 4	Eb Minor
	b motive	5 - 9	Eb Minor
	a interlude	9 - 10	Eb Minor
	b motive	11 – 15	Gb Minor
	a motive	15 – 18	Eb Minor
Theme II (B)	a motive (piano)/ c motive (violin)	19 – 39	Bb Min/Eb Min
	b motive	47 – 51	Eb Minor
	a motive	52 – 53	Gb Minor
	b motive	54 – 56	Eb Minor
Bridge	b motive	57 – 58	Bb Minor
Theme (Varied)		59 – 67	Eb Minor
	d interlude	67 – 68	Eb Major
Themes I & II		69 – 76	Eb Major
Coda	a motive	77 – 86	Eb Minor

[Sample No. 1: APA-style Table]

The third movement, *"Adagio Mesto,"* initially appears to have little formal structure, but upon closer examination, there is a high degree of formal structure. The overall form of the movement is ABA, but it could also be viewed as having a sonata-allegro form. There are two themes that have expositions, a development section, and a recapitulation of the first theme, which returns to the home key of EI minor and ends with a coda. Table 3.14 outlines the form of the movement.

Table 3.14

Brahms, Trio for violin, horn, and piano, Op. 40, Mvt. 3, Form

Sections	Subsections	Measures	Keys
Theme I (A)	a motive	1 - 4	E♭ Minor
	b motive	5 - 9	E♭ Minor
	a interlude	9 - 10	E♭ Minor
	b motive	11 – 15	G♭ Minor
	a motive	15 – 18	E♭ Minor
Theme II (B)	a motive (piano)/ c motive (violin)	19 – 39	B♭ Min/E♭ Min
	b motive	47 – 51	E♭ Minor
	a motive	52 – 53	G♭ Minor
	b motive	54 – 56	E♭ Minor
Bridge	b motive	57 – 58	B♭ Minor
Theme (Varied)		59 – 67	E♭ Minor
	d interlude	67 – 68	E♭ Major
Themes I & II		69 – 76	E♭ Major
Coda	a motive	77 – 86	E♭ Minor

[Sample No. 2: Turabian-style Table]

To determine whether differences in downbeat note placements were significantly different among the three performers, a
one-way ANOVA without replications was computed for all
downbeat note placements (beat subdivisions 1.0, 2.0, 3.0, and
4.0). The results are summarized in Table 11. The analysis indicated statistically significant differences among the three performers' downbeat note placements.

Table 11. Analysis of Variance: Comparison of Downbeat Note
Placements Among Three Performers

Source	SS	df	MS	F	p
Between Performers	329873.40	2	146936.70	105.79	<.001
Within Performers	1747813.35	1121	1559.16		
Total	2077686.74	1123			

[Sample No. 2: APA-style Table]

To determine whether differences in downbeat note placements were significantly different among the three performers, a
one-way ANOVA without replications was computed for all
downbeat note placements (beat subdivisions 1.0, 2.0, 3.0, and
4.0). The results are summarized in Table 11. The analysis indicated statistically significant differences among the three performers' downbeat note placements.

Table 11

*Analysis of Variance: Comparison of Downbeat Note Placements Among
Three Performers*

Source	*SS*	*df*	*MS*	*F*	*p*
Between Performers	329873.40	2	146936.70	105.79	<.001
Within Performers	1747813.35	1121	1559.16		
Total	2077686.74	1123			

APPENDIX J
Sample Figures

[Sample No. 1: Turabian-style Figure]

Each eight-measure excerpt was digitally recorded, allowing measurement to the nearest hundredth of a second for each right-hand chord (see Figure 1). An examination of each artist's recording revealed that gestures were played with a high level of consistency within each recording. Cultural or linguistic influences may have contributed to the rythmic approach of each artist.

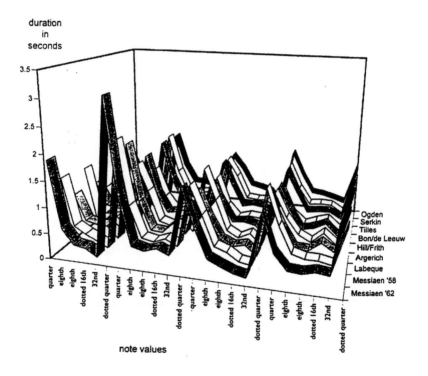

Figure 1. Timing profiles of the right-hand chords of the first eight measures of the fourth movement solo. The performers are listed at the right.

[Sample No. 1: APA-style Figure]

Each eight-measure excerpt was digitally recorded, allowing measurement to the nearest hundredth of a second for each right-hand chord (see Figure 1). An examination of each artist's recording revealed that gestures were played with a high level of consistency within each recording. Cultural or linguistic influences may have contributed to the rythmic approach of each artist.

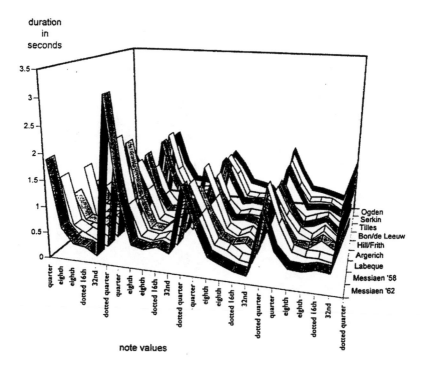

Figure 1. Timing profiles of the right-hand chords for the first eight measures of the fourth movement solo. The performers are listed at the right.

[Sample No. 2: Turabian-style Figure]

The mix session had two tasks to accomplish. The first was to balance and pan the music, and the second was to balance the voice over with the music. Reverb and chorus effects and settings, from the Yamaha 02R mixer, were used for the acoustic guitar (see Figure 1.4 and Figure 1.5).

REV STAGE

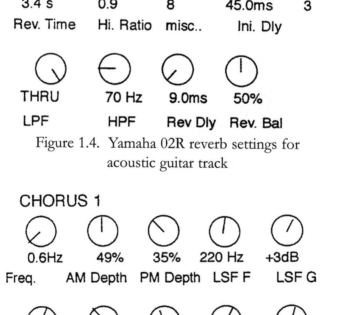

Figure 1.4. Yamaha 02R reverb settings for acoustic guitar track

CHORUS 1

Figure 1.5. Yamaha 02R chorus settings for acoustic guitar track

[Sample No. 2: APA-style Figure]

The mix session had two tasks to accomplish. The first was to balance and pan the music, and the second was to balance the voice over with the music. Reverb and chorus effects and settings, from the Yamaha 02R mixer, were used for the acoustic guitar (see Figure 1.4 and Figure 1.5).

REV STAGE

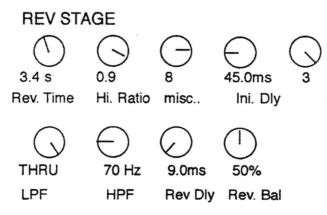

Figure 1.4. Yamaha 02R reverb settings for acoustic guitar track

CHORUS 1

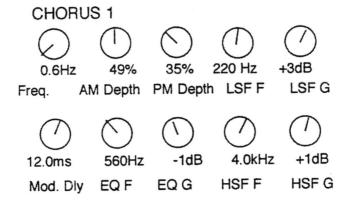

Figure 1.5. Yamaha 02R chorus settings for acoustic guitar track